+

HEY

JUDE

Johnny A Palmer Jr.

Book of Jude

(Spiritual Survivor Man Series)

Content

Introduction

These studies are not designed to be exhaustive by any means, but then, neither should they be considered mere bones of an outline. After pastoring for well over 30 years I have preached enough sermons to choke a horse and without a doubt some of my sermons could have gagged a tough old mule! My hope is this will help fellow pastors and believers to learn and enjoy studying the Bible. I confess I am addicted to both illustrations and alliteration but it is helpful in keeping things interesting and remembering what has been studied. My goal is to glorify God! I remember reading somewhere about a man who went to hear one preacher after another. Leaving he said to himself, "My oh my, what a preacher!" Then he heard Charles Haddon Spurgeon and left with tears streaming down his face saying, "My oh my, what a Savior!" If when you're finished with this book you say, "My what a wonderful preacher" then I have failed miserable in my purpose. It is my prayer that when you put this book down you could cry out, "My, what a precious Savior the Lord Jesus Christ truly is!" We are all familiar with the Beatles, and their song *Hey Jude*, here is the song rewritten by me for the introduction of this book.

Hey Jude, no need to stay bad
Take the Savior in and He will make it better.
Remember to receive Him into your heart
Then He'll start to make your life better.
Hey, Jude says don't be afraid
You were made by God and who could know you better?
The minute you let Jesus into your heart,
Then He will start to make you better.
And anytime you feel the pain, just read Jude, again and again
And you'll stop trying to carry the world upon your shoulder.
For well you know that it's a fool who lets self rule
By making his world, by his own little power.
Yah, yah, yah, yah, yah, yah, yah, yah, yah,
Hey, Jude says, this letter won't let you down
Because it's God's Word, and there's nothing better.
Remember all we need to do is let Him into our hearts.
Now, what in time or eternity could be better.
So let Him into your heart and life will begin.

You don't have to be waiting for someone to perform
Because God will do that for you, says Jude. He'll do
The power you need is on His shoulder.
Yah, yah, yah, yah, yah, yah, yah, yah, yah,
Hey, Jude says, don't remain bad
Take in the Savior, as He alone can make your life better.
Remember to let Him, the Lord Jesus, into heart and win.
He will forgive your sin
Then things could not be better.
Better, better, better, better, better, oh
Yah, yah, yah, yah, yah, yah, yah, yah, yah,
Yah, yah, yah, yah, yah, yah, yah, yah, yah,

I know, I won't quit my day job, but always wanted to do something like that. Anyway I hope this little study is a blessing to you and brings much glory and praise to the Lord Jesus Christ.

Chapter One

A Descriptive Greeting

¹ Jude, a bond-servant of Jesus Christ, and brother of James, To those who are the called, beloved in God the Father, and kept for Jesus Christ: ² May mercy and peace and love be multiplied to you. Jude 1:1-2

The Nelson Study Bible notes, "Few books in the N.T. have more to say to our generation than the Epistle of Jude. Distorters of the faith will find the book distasteful because of its warnings and uncompromising stance against defectors from the truth of Jesus Christ. But to those who approach the book with receptive hearts, Jude's words speak as clearly and forcefully today as they did almost two thousand years ago."

This is a small but powerful book. The *Descriptive* Greeting begins with the Author and his Audience.

The Author

JUDE'S *IDENTITY*

Jude – it is literally Judas or Judah. The name Jude (Judas) is the Greek form of the well-known Old Testament Hebrew name Judah. The title of the book is *Hey Jude*, bringing back a nostalgic moment, for those Beatle fans. It is designed to catch people's attention; a preacher does what a preacher has to do! The term has 6 distinct uses in the New Testament. Specifically, it refers:

- to Judah, the son of Jacob in the genealogy of Jesus (Matthew 1:2);
- to Judah, one of the 12 tribes of Israel (Revelation 5:5; 7:5);
- to Judah, the southern kingdom after the division (Hebrews 7:14; 8:8);
- to Judas Iscariot, the thief who betrayed Jesus and committed suicide (Matthew 27:3ff.; John 12:4ff.);
- to Judas, the son (brother, cf. KJV) of James [Greek text, just says lit., "of James.", who was one of the 12 apostles (Luke 6:16);
- to Judas, the brother of the Lord (Mark 6:3) who authored the general epistle known as Jude.

JUDE'S RECEPTION OF *MERCY*

This dude is Jude, but not Judas Iscariot!

Charles Spurgeon notes:

"This Judas was not the son of perdition, but a true son of God, a sincere and earnest-hearted believer. Yet, when he wrote his own name down, Judas, which we pronounce short as "Jude," I think that the tears must have come to his eyes as he remembered that other Judas,-with the same name, and by birth with the same nature. If left to himself, he might have proved a traitor to his Master, like the other Judas; but grace had made him to differ from the man who betrayed his Lord. If it had been your case or mine, I am sure that we could not have written down that name without reflecting upon our obligations to the sovereign grace of God, which kept us from being sons of perdition."

How many Johnny Palmer's will die and go to hell? People who have the same name as I do, and the same sin nature as me, and with my same condition of spiritual death. Why will I end up in heaven instead of the lake of fire?

God's Grace! There is an old saying that is true, "But for the grace of God there go I!" I think most of us feel like John Newton who said:

"When I get to heaven I shall see three wonders there. The first wonder will be, to see many people there whom I did not expect to see—the second wonder will be, to miss many people whom I did expect to see; and the third and greatest wonder of all, will be to find myself there."

Ken Langley shares this amusing story, "After worrying for half an hour that we wouldn't get on an overbooked flight, my wife and I were summoned to the check-in desk. A smiling agent whispered that this was our lucky day. To get us on the plane he was bumping us up to first class. This was the first and only time we've been so pampered on an airplane—good food, hot coffee, plenty of elbow-room. We played a little game, trying to guess who else didn't belong in first class. One man stuck out. He padded around the cabin in his socks, restlessly sampling magazines, playing with but never actually using the in-flight phones. Twice he sneezed so loudly we thought the oxygen masks would drop down. And when the attendant brought linen tablecloths for our breakfast trays, he tucked his into his collar as a bib. We see misfits at church, too—people who obviously don't belong, people who embarrass us and cause us to feel superior. The truth is we don't belong there any more than they do."

JUDE'S *SLAVERY*

a bond-servant – the Greek word is not *diakonos* "[household servant"] but *doulos*. The word obviously indicates Jude's submission to the Lord. Barclay notes:

- To call the Christian the *doulos* of God means that he is inalienably possessed by God. In the ancient world a master possessed his slaves in the same sense as he possessed his tools. A servant can change his master; but a slave cannot. The Christian inalienably belongs to God.

- To call the Christian the *doulos* of God means that he is unqualifiedly at the disposal of God. In the ancient world the master could do what he liked with his slave. He had the same power over his slave as he had over his inanimate possessions. He had the power of life and death over his slave. The Christian belongs to God, for God to send him where He will, and to do with him what He will. The Christian is the man who has no rights of his own, for all his rights are surrendered to God.

- To call the Christian the *doulos* of God means that the Christian owes an unquestioning obedience to God. Ancient law was such that a master's command was a slave's only law. Even if a slave was told to do something which actually broke the law, he could not protest, for as far as he was concerned, his master's command was the law. In any situation the Christian has but one question to ask: "Lord, what wilt *Thou* have me to do?" The command of God is his only law.

- To call the Christian the *doulos* of God means that he must be constantly in the service of God. In the ancient world the slave had literally no time of his own, no holidays, no time off, no working-hours settled by agreement, no leisure.

All his time belonged to the master. Every believer is to be a free will slave of Christ.

"And now, Lord, take note of their threats, and grant that your bond-servants may speak Your word with all confidence. Acts 4:29

"Following after Paul and us, she kept crying out, saying, "These men are bond-servants of the Most High God, who are proclaiming to you the way of salvation." Acts 16:17

"Paul, a bond-servant of Christ Jesus, called as an apostle, set apart for the gospel of God," Romans 1:1

"just as you learned it from Epaphras, our beloved fellow bond-servant, who is a faithful servant of Christ on our behalf," Colossians 1:7

"The Revelation of Jesus Christ, which God gave Him to show to His bond-servants, the things which must soon take place; and He sent and communicated it by His angel to His bond-servant John," Revelation 1:1

"19 Or do you not know that your body is a temple of the Holy Spirit who is in you, whom you have from God, and that you are not your own? 20 For you have been bought with a price: therefore glorify God in your body."
1 Corinthians 6:19-20

John MacArthur observes, "In the Greco-Roman world slavery was widespread, making the familiar New Testament designation bond-servant very significant. It denoted being owned and rendering absolute, selfless submission to someone, in this case to Jesus as Lord. In this letter such identification is especially fitting because it sets Jude in sharp contrast to the apostates. He was a grateful, willing slave of the Lord Jesus Christ, whereas the apostates denied Christ's lordship through their overtly sinful lifestyles. (v. 4; cf. 2 Peter 2:1)."

The picture is of a wild unbroken horse that wants its independence. It does not want to be ridden; it does not want to be told what to do or where to go. Oh, it accepts it when the cowboy feeds it or gives it plenty of water to drink. It will gladly receive the stable built to keep it out of the rain. It just says just don't get on my back, Jack! But the process of turning that horse into a useful stallion involves breaking the stallion so as to allow Jack to get on his back and direct it's going and coming. It is not a pleasant process; it always involves a lot of bucking, biting, and brings Jack to the ground level. If the horse could talk he is repeatedly communicating, "Stay off my back, Jack!" But our good cowboy will not be dissuaded from his planned purpose. When the goal is reached it becomes a thing of beauty, and something that God created the stallion to be from the beginning. Many of us want the blessings from God, but we don't want Him riding us and bringing us into submission to His will. That simply won't do!

We should also keep in mind that this word also includes the idea of honor. The great leaders of God's people in the Old Testament were also called "servants" of God, such as:

- Abraham (Ps 105:42);
- Moses (Josh. 14:7; 2 Kings 18:12);
- David (Ps. 18:1; Ezek. 34:23);
- and Daniel (Dan 6:20).

Also, to say that Jude is a slave of Jesus Christ indicates that Jesus Christ is in the position of Lord or an acknowledgement that He is God. The phrase, "servant of the Lord" or "servant of God" is a standard Old Testament phrase. When Jude puts "Jesus Christ" in place of "the Lord" or "God," then, he is communicating something of immense importance about Jesus—that He has a relationship to Jude similar to the relationship of the Lord to Moses and David. As one noted:

"This was an amazing step for a Jew like Jude, steeped in his people's strict monotheism. But his associating Jesus with God is all the more impressive when we remember that Jude had grown up in the same household as Jesus. Surely an event as spectacular as the Resurrection was necessary to have led Jude to view his own brother as one who was in some sense equal to God...We must, of course not imagine that he had worked out all the theological implications inherent in speaking of Jesus in these terms...But early Christians had an experience of Jesus that led them to begin applying to him language they had in the past reserved for God. Only gradually did they work out the theological implications of this transfer of language. But the point is that we need somehow to "hear" these theological overtones in the language Jude uses if we are fully to appreciate the significance of what he says...Once we recognize the theological overtones in the phrase "servant of Jesus Christ," we can find in the phrase a reminder of the exalted nature of Jesus. His exalted status is something that, after centuries of orthodox teaching, most of us take for granted. But many do not, and many who do give Him a unique status fail to give him "equal billing" with God the Father (e.g., Jehovah's Witnesses; Mormons)."

What Jude hints at, other Scriptures have made crystal clear: John 1:1; 20:28; Romans 9:5; 2 Peter 1:1; Titus 2:13.

- They *Praised* him (e.g., Matt. 14:33; 28:9, 17; cf. Heb. 1:6);
- They *Pointed* to Old Testament verses about Yahweh to him (e.g., Rom. 10:13);
- They *Prayed* to him (e.g., Acts 7:59).

JUDE'S *CHRISTOLOGY*

of Jesus Christ - Christ is not His last name! It is Jesus the Christ, the Messiah, the Anointed One. We have the special *Revelation* afforded Jude, I mean he grew up with Jesus. How cool would that be!

"54 He came to His hometown and began teaching them in their synagogue, so that they were astonished, and said, "Where did this man get this wisdom and these miraculous powers? 55 "Is not this the carpenter's son? Is not His mother called Mary, and His brothers, James and Joseph and Simon and Judas [Jude]? Matthew 13:54-55

Yet in spite of awesome privilege we see Jude's *Rejection.*

"1 After these things Jesus was walking in Galilee, for He was unwilling to walk in Judea because the Jews were seeking to kill Him. 2 Now the feast of the Jews, the Feast of

Booths, was near. 3 Therefore, His brothers said to Him, "Leave here and go into Judea, so that Your disciples also may see Your works which You are doing. 4 "For no one does anything in secret when he himself seeks to be known publicly. If You do these things, show Yourself to the world." 5 For not even His brothers were believing in Him. John 7:1-5

But as I always tell my wife, Ann, all ends well, that ends well, so we also see his *Recognition*. What caused Him to believe that Jesus was the Christ? Nothing short of the resurrection of the Lord Jesus Christ!

Warren Wiersbe observes, "Since the author of this epistle was the brother of James, this would make him the half brother of our Lord Jesus Christ (see Mark 6:3). Our Lord's brothers in the flesh did not believe in Him while He was ministering (John 7:5). But after the Resurrection, James was converted (see 1 Cor. 15:7), and we have every reason to believe that Jude was also saved at that time. Acts 1:14 informs us that "His brethren" were part of the praying group that was awaiting the Holy Spirit; 1 Corinthians 9:5 states that "the brethren of the Lord" were known in the early church."

John Philips, "None of the other children in Joseph and Mary's home were out of the ordinary. Jesus' sisters were just village girls. We would like to know more about them. His brothers—James, Joses, Simon, Judas—were nobodies too. In the end He won them all (Acts 1:12-14). James and Judas wrote books that found their way into the New Testament. James also became the leading elder of the Jerusalem church. It is difficult for us to picture those brothers and sisters growing up in the same family as the sinless Son of God and being so blind as not to see who He really was. He was so human. He played with them, went to the synagogue school with them, watched over them, protected them, helped them, wept with them, laughed with them, sang with them, prayed with them, and dearly loved them. After the resurrection the Lord personally appeared to James, maybe in the workshop at Nazareth (1 Corinthians 15:7). In any case, His resurrection blew away the cobwebs from their eyes."

The Resurrection makes the difference! Wilder shares, "I remember that after I had worked in university centers in Portugal I went from there to Norway, and I was a little impressed by the difference among the people. I wondered how one could explain it. Then I remembered that every representation I had seen in Portugal of Jesus Christ was that of as an infant in someone's arms, or else as crucified on the cross. But the first painting I saw on reaching Norway was that of the empty tomb, the three women and the angel. "He is not here; He is risen." The thought came to me, "May that not explain possibly some of the difference in the types of Christianity in Portugal and in Norway?"

"^{17} and if Christ has not been raised, your faith is worthless; you are still in your sins. ^{18} Then those also who have fallen asleep in Christ have perished. 19 If we have hoped in Christ in this life only, we are of all men most to be pitied." 1 Corinthians 15:17-19

JUDE'S *HUMILITY*

and brother of James –James, is the only man in the early church who could be called simply "James" with no risk of confusing anybody as to who he was. After the death of James the son of Zebedee, only one early Christian leader was commonly called simply "James," without the need for further identification (Acts 12:17; 15:13; 21:18; 1 Cor. 15:7; Gal 2:9, 12); And only one pair of brothers called James and Judas are known from the N.T. (Mark 6:3). Jude therefore uses this phrase to identify himself by reference to his more famous brother. Of course, he too must have been known to the churches he addresses, but Judas was too common a name, even among Christian leaders, to identify him alone (Cf. Luke 6:16; John 14:22; Acts 15:22). We should also note that the early church used the title "brother of the Lord", as a way of focusing on their uniqueness and authoritative position in the church. It appears that these brothers themselves were too humble to claim authority based merely on their physical relationship to Jesus, and thus seem to be uneasy with the term. The bottom line is, James and Jude were brothers - and half brothers of Jesus Christ. Our Lord of course was virgin born, but after He was born Mary and Joseph had children.

"Is not this the carpenter, the son of Mary, and brother of James and Joses and Judas and Simon? Are not His sisters here with us?" And they took offense at Him." Mark 6:3

"But I did not see any other of the apostles except James, the Lord's brother." Galatians 1:19

Jude could have added "and half-brother of Jesus" - the fact that he didn't reveals his humility. Jude was too humble to advertise Himself as the half-brother of Jesus Christ.

God loves humility in His children. The Bible tells us, "Whoever exalts himself shall be humbled; and whoever humbles himself shall be exalted." Matthew 23:12. See also Phil. 2:5-9.

A little boy was out fishing with only a switch for a pole and a bent pin for a hook, but he was catching many fish. A city slicker, who had spent the day fishing without catching a thing, came upon the boy with his long string of fish, and asked the boy the reason for his success. The boy said, "The secret of it all is that I keep myself out of sight." We too must keep ourselves out of sight so that people can see the Lord Jesus Christ, that is the only real success, giving God all the glory. So we have a brief Descriptive greeting about the Author.

Colton notes, "There are three difficulties in authorship: (1) to write anything worth publishing, (2)to find honest men to publish it, and (3) to get sensible men to read it." Well we have gotten past the first two difficulties - the book of Jude is certainly worth publishing since it is inspired by the Holy Spirit (2 Tim. 3:16-17); it was written by an honest man, in that he was writing under the inspiration of God; and now the only remaining difficulty is are we sensible enough to study this book week after week? I would suggest you open up the book of Jude and read it at least ten times just to get familiar with it. In the U.S. alone, a total of over 5 billion greeting cards are produced. Over $150 million are spent on postage to mail them. The smallest greeting card ever sent was to the Prince of Wales written on a grain of rice! We have looked at the Author and now we continue on with the Audience.

The Audience

The *Privileges* of the believer

We are *Called* by the Spirit

To those who are the called - Called out, invited, chosen, appointed. One of the names for the Holy Spirit is Paraclete. The Paraclete is "one who is called alongside." The church is ecclessia, lit. "the called-out ones." The church is called out of the world, unto fellowship with the Lord. Here is some interesting things to take note of:

- The called can be used for *Identification* of one's name.
  "She will bear a Son; and you shall call His name Jesus, for He will save His people from their sins." Matthew 1:21

- Can be used as a *Identification* title. Speaking of believers John writes, "See how great a love the Father has bestowed on us, that we would be called children of God; and such we are. For this reason the world does not know us, because it did not know Him." 1 John 3:1

- It can be used in the sense of an *Invitation*.
  "16 But He said to him, "A man was giving a big dinner, and he invited many; 17 and at the dinner hour he sent his slave to say to those who had been invited, 'Come; for everything is ready now.' 18 "But they all alike began to make excuses. The first one said to him, 'I have bought a piece of land and I need to go out and look at it; please consider me excused.' 19 "Another one said, 'I have bought five yoke of oxen, and I am going to try them out; please consider me excused.' 20 "Another one said, 'I have married a wife, and for that reason I cannot come.' 21 "And the slave came back and reported this to his master. Then the head of the household became angry and said to his slave, 'Go out at once into the streets and

lanes of the city and bring in here the poor and crippled and blind and lame.' 22 "And the slave said, 'Master, what you commanded has been done, and still there is room.' 23 "And the master said to the slave, 'Go out into the highways and along the hedges, and compel them to come in, so that my house may be filled. 24 'For I tell you, none of those men who were invited shall taste of my dinner.'" Luke 14:16-24

- It can be used in legal *Indictment*. "And when they had summoned them, they commanded them not to speak or teach at all in the name of Jesus." Acts 4:18

- Believers are called to special *Endowment*.
"Paul, a bond-servant of Christ Jesus, called as an apostle, set apart for the gospel of God," Romans 1:1

- Believers are called to live *Irenical* lives. "13 And a woman who has an unbelieving husband, and he consents to live with her, she must not send her husband away. 14 For the unbelieving husband is sanctified through his wife, and the unbelieving wife is sanctified through her believing husband; for otherwise your children are unclean, but now they are holy. 15 Yet if the unbelieving one leaves, let him leave; the brother or the sister is not under bondage in such cases, but God has called us to peace." 1 Corinthians 7:13-15

- In our passage it is related to the call to *Initial* salvation:
  "28 And we know that God causes all things to work together for good to those who love God, to those who are called according to His purpose. 29 For those whom He foreknew, He also predestined to become conformed to the image of His Son, so that He would be the firstborn among many brethren; 30 and these whom He predestined, He also called; and these whom He called, He also justified; and these whom He justified, He also glorified." Romans 8:28-30
  "23 And He did so to make known the riches of His glory upon vessels of mercy, which He prepared beforehand for glory, 24 even us, whom He also called, not from among Jews only, but also from among Gentiles. 25 As He

says also in Hosea, "I WILL CALL THOSE WHO WERE NOT MY PEOPLE, 'MY PEOPLE,' AND HER WHO WAS NOT BELOVED, 'BELOVED.'" 26 "AND IT SHALL BE THAT IN THE PLACE WHERE IT WAS SAID TO THEM, 'YOU ARE NOT MY PEOPLE,' THERE THEY SHALL BE CALLED SONS OF THE LIVING GOD." Romans 9:23-26

God's call is:

- *Universal*. Paul told the men of Athens that God "now commands all men everywhere" to repent (Acts 17:30). Jn. 3:16 tells us that "God so loved the world, that he gave his only begotten Son, that whosoever believeth in him should not perish, but have everlasting life." This universal call often is rejected, "Jerusalem, Jerusalem, who kills the prophets and stones those who are sent to her! How often I wanted to gather your children together, the way a hen gathers her chicks under her wings, and you were unwilling. Matthew 23:37
  James Kennedy, "The Bible speaks of both a calling which is effectual, and a calling which is not. If anyone should respond to that calling, they would

receive eternal life because God will refuse no one...But there is a problem. Man in his fallen condition is so bound by sin and blinded by his iniquity that he desires to have nothing to do with the holy God because his heart is at enmity with God...Man is always free to do what he wants to do, that's why he is responsible for everything he does. But, he doesn't have the power or the desire to do what he ought to do."

- The call becomes *individual* when it is brought to us.

- It becomes *personal* when we receive it. "Come to Me, all who are weary and heavy-laden, and I will give you rest. Matthew 11:28
"The Spirit and the bride say, "Come." And let the one who hears say, "Come." And let the one who is thirsty come; let the one who wishes take the water of life without cost." Revelation 22:17

No one among fallen humanity initiates seeking after God.

"9 What then? Are we better than they? Not at all; for we have already charged that both Jews and Greeks are all under sin; 10 as it is written, "THERE IS NONE RIGHTEOUS, NOT EVEN ONE; 11 THERE IS NONE WHO UNDERSTANDS, THERE IS NONE WHO SEEKS FOR GOD;" Romans 3:9-11

As one put it:

"I sought the Lord, and afterward I knew,
He moved my soul to seek Him, seeking me;
It was not I that found, O Savior true,
No I was found of Thee."

CBL, "It is always God who issues the call; the term election is never used of man choosing God, but of God choosing man. The Bible teaches that none choose God because fallen man is spiritually dead."

The New American Commentary, "We will begin with the term "called." English readers, when asked to define the word "called," might give the definition "invited." Such a definition would misunderstand radically what Jude intended. The term "called" does not merely mean that God invited believers to be His own. Those whom God calls are powerfully and inevitably brought to faith in Jesus Christ through the proclamation of the gospel. The call of God is extended only to some and is always successful, so that all those who are called become believers. Such an understanding of "called" is clearly attested in the Pauline writings."

Why did Jude emphasize such an idea here? We need to recall that intruders had threatened the faith of the church. Jude, in the course of his letter, will give some sharp warnings to his readers. Such warnings, however, could give the impression that the focus is on human effort and endurance. Jude, by stressing God's supernatural calling, reminds the readers of the efficacy of God's grace." Now personally I am not a doctrinal dueler – I am not one to argue the point. As someone said, "If a stick is crooked, there is no need to argue about it, just lay a straight stick beside it." I simply will let the straight Word of God speak for itself:

[1] Paul, a bond-servant of Christ Jesus, called *as* an apostle, set apart for the gospel of God... [6] among whom you also are **the called of Jesus Christ**; [7] to all who are beloved of God in Rome, called *as* saints: Grace to you and peace from God our Father and the Lord Jesus Christ. Romans 1:1, 6-7

[1] Paul, **called** *as* an apostle of Jesus Christ **by the will of God**, and Sosthenes our brother, [2] To the church of God which is at Corinth, to those who have been sanctified in Christ Jesus, saints by calling, with all who in every place call on the name of our Lord Jesus Christ, their *Lord* and ours:…[9] **God is faithful, through whom you were called** into fellowship with His Son, Jesus Christ our Lord… [24] but to those who are the called, both Jews and Greeks, Christ the power of God and the wisdom of God." 1 Corinthians 1:2, 9, 24

[15] But when God, who had set me apart *even* from my mother's womb and **called me through His grace**, was pleased. Galatians 1:15

[12] so that you would walk in a manner worthy of **the God who calls you** into His own kingdom and glory. 1 Thessalonians 2:12

[24] Faithful is **He who calls you**, and He also will bring it to pass. 1 Thessalonians 5:24

[14] It was for this **He called you** through our gospel, that you may gain the glory of our Lord Jesus Christ. 2 Thessalonians 2:14

[9] But you are A CHOSEN RACE, A royal PRIESTHOOD, A HOLY NATION, A PEOPLE FOR

God's OWN POSSESSION, so that you may proclaim the excellencies **of Him who has called you** out of darkness into His marvelous light; 1 Peter 2:9

[10] After you have suffered for a little while, the God of all grace, **who called you** to His eternal glory in Christ, will Himself perfect, confirm, strengthen *and* establish you. 1 Peter 5:10

[3] seeing that His divine power has granted to us everything pertaining to life and godliness, through the true **knowledge of Him who called us** by His own glory and excellence. 2 Peter 1:3

[14] "These will wage war against the Lamb, and the Lamb will overcome them, because He is Lord of lords and King of kings, and those who are with Him *are the* **called** and chosen and faithful." Revelation 17:14

The NIV Application Commentary, "Jude identifies his readers as Christians. The key word in the description is "called" (*kletois*). This word reflects the New Testament conviction that being a Christian is a product of God's gracious reaching out to bring helpless sinners into a relationship with himself. "Call"... means "choose" or "select," and God's "choosing"—because it is he, the sovereign Lord, who is doing it—is effective. All this lies in the background."

"12 But as many as received Him, to them He gave the right to become children of God, even to those who believe in His name, 13 who were born, not of blood nor of the will of the flesh nor of the will of man, **but of God**." John 1:12-13

"You did not choose Me but **I chose you**, and appointed you that you would go and bear fruit, and that your fruit would remain, so that whatever you ask of the Father in My name He may give to you." John 15:16

"20 "For the Father loves the Son, and shows Him all things that He Himself is doing; and the Father will show Him greater works than these, so that you will marvel. 21 "For just as the Father raises the dead and gives them life, even so the Son also **gives life to whom He wishes**." John 5:20-21

"A woman named Lydia, from the city of Thyatira, a seller of purple fabrics, a worshiper of God, was listening; and **the Lord opened her heart** to respond to the things spoken by Paul." Acts 16:14

"No one can come to Me **unless** the Father who sent Me draws him" (John 6:44; cf.v. 65).

"Therefore do not be ashamed of the testimony of our Lord or of me His prisoner, but join with me in suffering for the gospel according to the power of God, who has saved us and **called us** with a holy calling, not according to our works, but **according to His own purpose and grace** which was granted us in Christ Jesus from all eternity. (2 Tim. 1:8-9)

John MacArthur, "In His sovereign wisdom, God chose believers based solely on His gracious purpose in Christ from before time began. His call, was not rooted in anything, He saw in them—not even their foreseen faith. Rather, His call was motivated by His own glory and good pleasure, that His mercy might be eternally put on display (Rom. 9:23-24). Believers, then, are those who are divinely elected to salvation. They did not earn God's choice; nor can they lose it or have it taken away (cf. John 6:37-40; 10:27- 30; Rom. 8:28-30, 38-39). Thus, they can rest in the security of God's gracious call, even in the most dangerous conflict with false teaching."

God always initiates the call to salvation. The Expository Dictionary of Bible Words notes:

"klētos is an adjective derived from the verb kaleō (see above), found eleven times with the meaning "called." The state of being "called" by God, implying sovereign divine election in the context of salvation, is indicated in Matt. 20:16; 22:14; Rom. 1:6 ff.; 8:28; Jude 1; Rev. 17:14." Charles Spurgeon observed, "...Salvation is of the Lord. I cannot find in Scripture any other doctrine than this. It is the essence of the Bible. Tell me anything contrary to this truth, and it will be a heresy; tell me a heresy and I shall find its essence here, that it has departed from this great, this fundamental, this rock-truth - God is my Rock and my Salvation. What is the heresy of Rome, but the addition of something to the perfect merits of Jesus Christ - the bringing in of the works of the flesh, to assist in our justification?...Every heresy, if brought to the touch stone, will discover itself here." This work is that of the Holy Spirit, the Westminster Confession: "Effectual calling is the work of God's Spirit, whereby, convincing us of our sin and misery, enlightening our mind in the knowledge of Christ, and renewing our wills, He does persuade and enable us to embrace Jesus Christ, freely offered to us in the Gospel."

We could speak of:

- Called with a Heavenly calling (Heb.3:1)
- Called for His purpose (Romans 8:28).

- Called to Have fellowship with Christ (1 Cor. 1:9).
- Called to Harmony. (1 Corinthians 7:15).
- Called to Have freedom. (Galatians 5:13).
- Called to a Hope. (Ephesians 4:4).
- Called to a High calling (Philippians 3:14).
- Called to Holiness. (2 Tim.1:9/1 Peter 1:15).
- Called to Inherit a blessing (1 Peter 3:9).
- Called to eternal Honor. (1 Peter 5:10).

Now that God has called us, it is our responsibility to walk worthy of that calling. "I therefore, the prisoner of the Lord, beseech you that ye walk worthy of the vocation wherewith ye are called." (Ephesians 4:1)

Believers are called:

1. "Children" for kinship—1 John 3:1, 2, R.V.
2. "Saints" for holiness—1 Cor. 1:2.
3. "Christians" for identification—Acts 11:26.
4. "Brethren" for fellowship—Heb. 2:11.
5. "Sheep" for character—John 10:3.
6. "Servants" for employment—Matt. xxv 14
7. "Friends" for companionship—John 15:15.

A member of a small church was asked to introduce the speaker at a Methodist evening church affair in Martinsville, Virginia. Because of bad weather the audience consisted of only a handful of people, but the man was equal to the occasion. He said, "I have been asked to introduce our speaker to you this evening, This I am very glad to do. Ladies and gentlemen, this is Mr. John Brown. Mr. Brown, meet Mr. and Mrs. Rucker, Mr. and Mrs. Witten, Mr. Stowall, Miss Stowall...."

Jude's greeting is not to a mega-church, a large audience of people but to every individual Christian. If you are a believer you have been called by God's Spirit to Salvation. Emily Post was born Emily Price in Baltimore, Maryland in 1873. She was the only daughter of famous architect Bruce Price and his wife Josephine Lee Price. She was educated at home and attended Miss Graham's finishing school in New York, where her family had moved. She married society banker Edwin Main Post in 1892 and had two sons. At the turn of the century, financial circumstances compelled her to begin writing to earn money, and she produced newspaper articles on architecture and interior design as well as stories and serials for such magazines as Harper's. She wrote on different topics, but her 1922 book "Etiquette" became a best seller and soon her articles on etiquette appeared in more than 200 newspapers. Someone once asked Emily: "What is the correct procedure when one is invited to the White House and has a previous engagement?" She answered, "An invitation to lunch or dine at the White House is a command, and automatically cancels any other engagement." The same can be said when called by God, that it cancels out any other engagement, and becomes the irresistible focus of our life.

We are looking at the Descriptive Greeting; we have seen the Author and now continue under the Audience. We have seen that they are Called by the Spirit of God and now we continue with the fact they are Beloved by God the Father. In the 1980s, people shelled out thousands of dollars to own a potbellied pig, an exotic house pet imported from Vietnam. Their breeders claimed these mini-pigs were quite smart and would grow to only 40 pounds. Well, they were half right. The pigs were smart. But they had a tendency to grow to about 150 pounds and become quite aggressive. What do people do with an unwanted potbellied pig? Fortunately, Dale Riffle came to the rescue. Someone had given Riffle one of these pigs, and he fell in love with it. The pig, Rufus, never learned to use its litter box and developed this craving for carpets and wallpaper and drywall. Yet Riffle sold his suburban home and moved with Rufus to a five-acre farm in West Virginia. He started taking in other unwanted pigs, and before long, the guy was living in hog heaven.

There are currently 180 residents on his farm. According to an article in U.S. News & World Report, they snooze on beds of pine shavings. They wallow in mud puddles. They soak in plastic swimming pools and listen to piped-in classical music. And they never need fear that one day they'll become bacon or pork chops. There's actually a waiting list of unwanted pigs trying to get a hoof in the door at Riffle's farm. Dale Riffle told the reporter, "We're all put on earth for some reason, and I guess pigs are my lot in life." How could anybody in his right mind fall in love with a pig! I'll tell you something even more amazing. An infinite, perfectly holy, majestic, awesome God is passionately in love with insignificant, sinful, openly rebellious, people - people like you and me.

We are *Beloved* by God the Father

A *PARENTAL* LOVE

"20 He got right up and went home to his father. "When he was still a long way off, his father saw him. His heart pounding, he ran out, embraced him, and kissed him. 21 The son started his speech: 'Father, I've sinned against God, I've sinned before you; I don't deserve to be called your son ever again.' 22 "But the father wasn't listening. He was calling to the servants, 'Quick. Bring a clean set of clothes and dress him. Put the family ring on his finger and sandals on his feet. 23 Then get a grain-fed heifer and roast it. We're going to feast! We're going to have a wonderful time! 24 My son is here—given up for dead and now alive! Given up for lost and now found!' And they began to have a wonderful time." Luke 15:20-24 (MSG)

Country singer George Strait sings a song entitled, "Love without End, Amen." It tells the story of a young boy coming home from school after having a fight and expecting punishment from his dad. Fully expecting the wrath of his father, the son waited, expecting the worst. However, the father said, "Let me tell you a secret about a father's love . . . Daddies don't just love their children every now and then . . . it's a love without end. Amen." The young lad grew up and passed this secret on to his children. One day he dreamed that he died and went to heaven. He was concerned, as he waited to go in, because he realized there must be some mistake for if they knew half the things he's done they would never let him in. It was then that he heard his father's words again, "Let me tell you a secret about a father's love . . . Daddies don't just love their children every now and then . . . it's a love without end. Amen." If you are God's child, then God's word clearly teaches that we have a Father like this!

A *SACRIFICIAL* LOVE

Jn. 3:16 says it all! See also Rom. 5:8

"In this is love, not that we loved God, but that He loved us and sent His Son to be the propitiation for our sins." 1 John 4:10

On August 16, 1987, Northwest Airlines flight 225 crashed just after taking off from the Detroit airport, killing 155 people. One survived: a four-year-old from Arizona named Cecelia. Cecelia survived because, even as the plane was falling, Cecelia's mother, Paula Chican, unbuckled her own seat belt, got down on her knees in front of her daughter, wrapped her arms and body around Cecelia, and then would not let her go. Such is the love of our Savior for us. He left heaven, lowered himself to us, and covered us with the sacrifice of his own body to save us.

IT IS *ETERNAL*

"Beloved" - translates a perfect passive participle derived from the familiar verb agapaō. The perfect tense indicates that God placed His love on believers in eternity past:

4 just as He chose us in Him before the foundation of the world, that we would be holy and blameless before Him. In love 5 He predestined us to adoption as sons through Jesus Christ to Himself, according to the kind intention of His will. Ephesians 1:4-5

With the results, that the action continue in the present and into the future - a love that will never end!

Now before the Feast of the Passover, Jesus knowing that His hour had come that He would depart out of this world to the Father, having loved His own who were in the world, He loved them to the end. John 13:1

35 Do you think anyone is going to be able to drive a wedge between us and Christ's love for us? There is no way! Not trouble, not hard times, not hatred, not hunger, not homelessness, not bullying threats, not backstabbing, not even the worst sins listed in Scripture: 36 They kill us in cold blood because

they hate you. We're sitting ducks; they pick us off one by one. [37] None of this fazes us because Jesus loves us. [38] I'm absolutely convinced that nothing—nothing living or dead, angelic or demonic, today or tomorrow, [39] high or low, thinkable or unthinkable—absolutely nothing can get between us and God's love because of the way that Jesus our Master has embraced us."
Romans 8:35-39 (MSG)

If it's eternally past and eternally future - then it is eternally now! In his book Enjoying God, Lloyd Ogilvie writes:

"My formative years ingrained into my attitude toward myself: do and you'll receive; perform and you'll be loved. When I got good grades, achieved, and was a success, I felt acceptance from my parents. My dad taught me to fish and hunt and worked hard to provide for us, but I rarely heard him say, "Lloyd, I love you." He tried to show it in actions, and sometimes I caught a twinkle of affirmation in his eyes. But I still felt empty. When I became a Christian, I immediately became so involved in discipleship activities that I did not experience the profound healing of the grace I talked about theoretically....I'll never forget as long as I live the first time I really experienced healing grace. I was a postgraduate student at the University of Edinburgh. Because of financial pressures I had to accordion my studies into a shorter than usual period. Carrying a double load of classes was very demanding, and I was exhausted by the constant feeling of never quite measuring up. No matter how good my grades were, I thought they could be better. Sadly, I was not living the very truths I was studying. Although I could have told you that the Greek words for grace and joy are charis and chara, I was not experiencing them. My beloved professor, Dr. James Stewart, saw into my soul with x-ray vision. One day in the corridor of New College he stopped me. He looked me in the eye intensely. Then he smiled warmly, took my coat lapels in his hands, drew me down to a few inches from his face, and said, "Dear boy, you are loved now!" God loves us now, not when we get better, but now, as we are!

IT IS *UNUSUAL*

"See how great a love the Father has bestowed on us, that we would be called children of God; and such we are" (1 John 3:1).

The expression rendered "how great" is from potapos, which originally meant, "From what

Country?" It describes divine love as something that is alien to human beings and outside their natural realm of understanding an other-worldly kind of love—as if it were a concept from a foreign culture or unknown race. None of us loved like God does, none of us, no not one!!! People do not usually love strangers; and they especially do not love their enemies (cf. Matt. 5:43-48). Yet, God chose to love sinners even when they were defiant sinners!

"1 It wasn't so long ago that you were mired in that old stagnant life of sin. 2 You let the world, which doesn't know the first thing about living, tell you how to live. You filled your lungs with polluted unbelief, and then exhaled disobedience. 3 We all did it, all of us doing what we felt like doing, when we felt like doing it, all of us in the same boat. It's a wonder God didn't lose his temper and do away with the whole lot of us. 4 Instead, immense in mercy and with an incredible love, 5 he embraced us. He took our sin-dead lives and made us alive in Christ. He did all this on his own, with no help from us! 6 Then he picked us up and set us down in highest heaven in company with Jesus, our Messiah." Ephesians 2:1-6 (MSG)

Although believers did nothing to gain His affection (and, in fact, did everything to invite His wrath), the Father loves redeemed sinners with the same love that He has for His Son... that is unusual! Out of the mouth of babes, I came across this true story:

The mother of a 9 yr. old boy named Mark received a phone call in the middle of the afternoon. It was the teacher from her son's school. "Mrs. Smith, something unusual happened today in your son's third-grade class. Your son did something that surprised me so much that I thought you should know about it. Nothing like this has happened in all my years of teaching. This morning I was teaching a lesson on creative writing. And as I always do, I tell the story of the ant and the grasshopper: "The ant works hard all summer and stores up plenty of food. But the grasshopper plays all summer and does no work. Then winter comes. The grasshopper begins to starve because he has no food. So he begs, 'Please Mr. Ant, you have much food. Please let me eat, too.'" Then I said, "Boys and girls, your job is to write the ending to the story."Your son, Mark, raised his hand. 'Teacher, may I draw a picture?' 'Well, yes, Mark, if you like, you may draw a picture. But first you must write the ending to the story.' "As in all the years past, most of the students said the ant shared his food through the winter, and both the ant and the grasshopper lived. A few children wrote, 'No, Mr. Grasshopper. You should have worked in the summer. Now I have just enough food for myself.' So the ant lived and the grasshopper died. "But your son ended the story in a way different from any other child, ever. He wrote, 'So the ant gave all of his food to the grasshopper; the grasshopper lived through the winter. But the ant died.' "And the picture? At the bottom of the page, Mark had drawn three crosses." That is unusual - not as unusual as God's love for us through Christ!

IT IS *UNCONDITONAL*

It is a passive voice meaning that we do not give but receive! Kenneth Wuest is helpful, "The participle is in the perfect tense, speaking of a past complete act having present, and in a context like this, permanent results. The distinctive word for "love" here is the word for God's self-sacrificial love which was shown at Calvary. This love here is the outgoing of God's love for the saints in which He gives of Himself for their good. He will do anything within His good will for the saints. He went all the way to Calvary for them when they were unlovely and naturally unlovable. He will do as much and more for His saints who in Christ are looked upon by God the Father with all the love with which He loves His Son. The perfect tense speaks here of the fact that the saints are the permanent objects of God's love. Jude is therefore writing to those who have been loved by God the Father with the present result that they are in a state of being the objects of His permanent love, and that love extends not merely through the brief span of this life, but throughout eternity. And then some dear children of God fear that they might be lost."

I have seen kids tease their dogs, pull their tails, even kick em and yet those dogs wagged their tails, licked their faces, expressed love regardless, that is just a dim picture of God's love for us!

6 Christ arrives right on time to make this happen. He didn't, and doesn't, wait for us to get ready. He presented himself for this sacrificial death when we were far too weak and rebellious to do anything to get ourselves ready. And even if we hadn't been so weak, we wouldn't have known what to do anyway. 7 We can understand someone dying for a person worth dying for, and we can understand how someone good and noble could inspire us to selfless sacrifice. 8 But God put his love on the line for us by offering his

Son in sacrificial death while we were of no use whatever to him. [9] Now that we are set right with God by means of this sacrificial death, the consummate blood sacrifice, there is no longer a question of being at odds with God in any way. [10] If, when we were at our worst, we were put on friendly terms with God by the sacrificial death of his Son, now that we're at our best, just think of how our lives will expand and deepen by means of his resurrection life! [11] Now that we have actually received this amazing friendship with God, we are no longer content to simply say it in plodding prose. We sing and shout our praises to God through Jesus, the Messiah!" Romans 5:6-11 (MSG)

All believers are Beloved in God! You say but I don't deserve it! I still sin! Yes...but the Father's love is based on placing you into Christ where you are forgiven and righteous, giving you eternal security and value! Here is a $10 bill. Who reading this book would like this $10 bill?" But what if this author crumples it up? Do you still want it? I am sure you would say, "Of course I want it!" But what if I throw it on the dirty ground and jump up and down on it – still want it? You bet! The lesson is that no matter what I do to this 10 bill, it is still worth 10 dollars. In the same way, many times in our lives, we are dropped, crumpled, and ground into the dirt by the decisions we make to sin. But no matter what has happened or what will happen, you will never lose your value in God's eyes. Dirty or clean, crumpled or finely creased, you are loved by God. No, this is not an encouragement to sin but actually a motivation to obedience with the right motive. We are Kept in, for, and by the Son of God. We have seen that we are Called by the Spirit of God; and Loved by God the Father; now we see we are Kept by the Son of God.

In one of those Superman movies, Superman saves a man from a burning building. He rescues him from the top floor and is carrying him to safety by flying through the skies. The man looks at Superman and then looks down to the ground. "I'm scared, Superman. Look how far down that is." Superman replies, "Now if I delivered you from the burning fire, what makes you think I am going to drop you when I'm carrying you to safety?" If God has delivered us from a burning hell, what makes us think He will drop us before He safely puts you down in our heavenly home?

We are *Kept* by the Lord Jesus

WE ARE *PRESERVED*

kept - expresses the idea of "to keep" with the sense of "preserve," in a number of different contexts this word refers to believers being kept or preserved for the coming of the Lord, the eternal inheritance for the people of God (1 Thess. 5:23; 1 John 5:18; Jude 1; 1 Pet. 1 :4)." [Expository Dictionary of Bible Words]

"Now may the God of peace Himself sanctify you entirely; and may your spirit and soul and body be preserved [kept] complete, without blame at the coming of our Lord Jesus Christ." 1 Thessalonians 5:23

"to obtain an inheritance which is imperishable and undefiled and will not fade away, reserved [having been kept] in heaven for you," 1 Peter 1:4

"We know that no one who is born of God sins; but He who was born of God keeps him, and the evil one does not touch him." 1 John 5:18

"Now to Him who is able to keep you from stumbling, and to make you stand in the presence of His glory blameless with great joy," Jude 1:24

We are preserved, kept, guarded, watched over by God - you cannot get any securer then that. Carnell Taylor was working on a paving crew repairing the Interstate 64 Bridge over the Elizabeth River in Virginia. The road was icy, and a pickup truck slid out of control and hit Taylor, knocking him off the bridge. He fell 70 feet and hit the cold waters of the river below. His pelvis and some of the bones in his face were broken. Joseph J. Brisson, the captain of a barge passing by at that moment, saw Taylor fall and quickly had to make a life-or-death decision. He knew Taylor would drown before he and his crew could launch their small boat and reach him. The numbingly cold water and strong currents of the river could kill him if he dived in to rescue Taylor. He had a family, and Christmas was three days away. Joseph decided to risk his life for a man he had never met. He dived into the river, swam to Taylor, and grabbed hold of him. "Don't worry, buddy," he said, "I got you." Brisson held Taylor's face above the water and encouraged him to keep talking. Then he took hold of a piece of wood in the water and slid it under Taylor to help keep him afloat. The current was too strong for them to swim to safety, and eventually the cold caused Brisson to lose his grip on Taylor. So Brisson wrapped his legs around the injured man's waist and held on. After nearly 30 minutes the crew from the barge was finally able to reach the two men and pull them from the water into the small boat. Taylor was hospitalized for broken bones. Joseph, the hero, was treated for mild hypothermia. He later told the Associated Press he knew what he had to do when he saw the man fall. "I have a family, I thought about that. But I thought about how life is very important. I'm a Christian man, and I couldn't let anything happen to him." Jesus is like that, He grabbed hold of us in salvation and is not about to let us go! He is not going to let anything happen to you!

IT IS A *PERFECT PARTICIPLE*

kept - the verb is a perfect participle, "having been kept." It means that we are kept at a point in time, with the results that we are continually kept. If you have been kept in the past, then you will be kept throughout eternity!

IT IS RELATED TO CHRISTS *PRAYER*

It is the same word found in John 17:11-12, 15.

"10 and all things that are Mine are Yours, and Yours are Mine; and I have been glorified in them. 11 "I am no longer in the world; and yet they themselves are in the world, and I come to You. Holy Father, keep them in Your name, the name which You have given Me, that they may be one even as We are. 12 "While I was with them, I was keeping them in Your name which You have given Me; and I guarded them and not one of them perished but the son of perdition, so that the Scripture would be fulfilled. John 17:10-12

""I do not ask You to take them out of the world, but to keep them from the evil one." John 17:15

Does God answer prayer? That's what I'm talking about!

ANSWERED PRAYER IS RELATED TO OUR *POSITION.*

*preserved **in** Christ* - is a possible translation. We were born In Adam and now we are In Christ, speaking of our place of security. In Adam there was nothing but condemnation; but there is no condemnation for those in Christ Jesus! I loved to watch the Crocodile man, Steve Erwin. Once he had built a cage and placed it in shark infested waters. No matter how aggressive the sharks became, no matter how close, he was perfectly safe as long as he stayed in that cage! Spirit baptism placed us safely in Christ!

"For by one Spirit we were all baptized into one body, whether Jews or Greeks, whether slaves or free, and we were all made to drink of one Spirit." 1 Corinthians 12:13

WE ARE SAVED FOR A *PURPOSE*

kept **for** *Jesus Christ* - NASB/AMB/ESV/WUEST
Not only is God our inheritance but we are His inheritance!

"I pray that the eyes of your heart may be enlightened, so that you will know what is the hope of His calling, what are the riches of the glory of His inheritance in the saints," Ephesians 1:18

We are His possession!

"But you are A CHOSEN RACE, A royal PRIESTHOOD, A HOLY NATION, A PEOPLE FOR God's OWN POSSESSION, so that you may proclaim the excellencies of Him who has called you out of darkness into His marvelous light;" 1 Peter 2:9

WE ARE KEPT BY HIS *POWER*

*kept **by** Jesus Christ* – this is another possible translation. Jacob was kept by God whereever he went, so are we!

""Behold, I am with you and will keep you wherever you go, and will bring you back to this land; for I will not leave you until I have done what I have promised you." Genesis 28:15

It is God's power that is keeping us alive at this moment. David confessed:

"O LORD, You have brought up my soul from Sheol; You have kept me alive, that I would not go down to the pit." Psalm 30:3

It is God's power that we are kept from sinning! God said to Abimelech:

"Then God said to him in the dream, "Yes, I know that in the integrity of your heart you have done this, and I also kept you from sinning against Me; therefore I did not let you touch her." Genesis 20:6

"The LORD will keep you from all evil; he will keep your life." Psalm 121:7 (ESV)

"Lo, for my own welfare I had great bitterness; It is You who has kept my soul from the pit of nothingness, For You have cast all my sins behind Your back." Isaiah 38:17

He is the one who keeps on giving us our daily food. Just like when Jesus fed the multitude, he feeds us individually day by day.

"Then He took the five loaves and the two fish, and looking up to heaven, He blessed them, and broke them, and kept giving them to the disciples to set before the people." Luke 9:16

The Lord is our keeper!

"5 The LORD is your keeper; The LORD is your shade on your right hand. 6 The sun will not smite you by day, Nor the moon by night." Psalm 121:5-6

Christ's Ability –"He Is Able" Eph. 3:20

- He is able to save to the uttermost, for He lives to do it, therefore rest in Him and be glad—Heb. 7:25.
- He is able to make all grace to abound towards us, therefore be satisfied with Him, and be thankful—2 Cor. 9:8-11.
- He is able to give us the victory when tempted, therefore take Him as Victor,

and be an overcomer—1 Cor. 10:13.

- He is able to keep us from falling, therefore lean upon Him and be upheld—Jude 24.
- He is able to shield us from harm, therefore abide in Him, and be at rest—Psa. 121:3-8.
- He is able to make us active, therefore let Him work effectively through us, and be useful—2 Tim. 1:12, R.V., margin.
- He is able to keep us always, therefore let Him tend us, and be fresh and sweet—Isa. 27:2, 3.

WE ARE KEPT BASED ON MANY *PROMISES*

- Undertakings Related to the *Father*:

  (1) The *Indisputable* sovereign purpose of God, which is unconditional. John 3:16 "Truly, truly, I say to you, he who hears My word, and believes Him who sent Me, has eternal life, and does not come into judgment, but has passed out of death into life." John 5:24 "36 "But I said to you that you have seen Me, and yet do not believe. 37 "All that the Father gives Me will come to Me, and the one who comes to Me I will certainly not cast out." John

6:36-37

(2) The *Infinite* power of God set free to save and keep.

"28 and I give eternal life to them, and they will never perish; and no one will snatch them out of My hand. 29 "My Father, who has given them to Me, is greater than all; and no one is able to snatch them out of the Father's hand." John 10:28-29 (NASB)

(3) The *Indescribable* love of God.

"just as He chose us in Him before the foundation of the world, that we would be holy and blameless before Him. In love." Ephesians 1:4

(4) The *Influence* on the Father of the prayer of the Son of God (cf. John 17:9-12, 15, 20).

- Undertakings Related to the *Son:*

  (1)His substitutionary death. Rom. 8:1 "1 My little children, I am writing these things to you so that you may not sin. And if anyone sins, we have an Advocate with the Father, Jesus Christ the righteous; 2 and He Himself is the propitiation for our sins; and not for ours only, but also for those of the whole world." 1 John 2:1-2

(2)His resurrection, securing a resurrection unto life for believers. "5 even when we were dead in our transgressions, made us alive together with Christ (by grace you have been saved), 6 and raised us up with Him, and seated us with Him in the heavenly places in Christ Jesus," Ephesians 2:5-6

(3) His advocacy, His intercession in heaven. 1 Jn. 2:2 "who is the one who condemns? Christ Jesus is He who died, yes, rather who was raised, who is at the right hand of God, who also intercedes for us." Romans 8:34 "Therefore He is able also to save forever those who draw near to God through Him, since He always lives to make intercession for them." Hebrews 7:25 "For Christ did not enter a holy place made with hands, a mere copy of the true one, but into heaven itself, now to appear in the presence of God for us;" Hebrews 9:24

- Undertakings Related to the *Spirit*:

(1)regeneration (partaking of the divine nature is entrance into that which cannot be removed;"4 But when the kindness of God our Savior and His

love for mankind appeared, 5 He saved us, not on the basis of deeds which we have done in righteousness, but according to His mercy, by the washing of regeneration and renewing by the Holy Spirit," Titus 3:4-5
(2)indwelling (He is given to abide forever and certainly by His presence the believer will be preserved; "I will ask the Father, and He will give you another Helper, that He may be with you forever;" John 14:16 "and hope does not disappoint, because the love of God has been poured out within our hearts through the Holy Spirit who was given to us." Romans 5:5
(3) baptism
(by which the believer is joined to Christ so as to share eternally in the New Creation glory and blessing;
"But the one who joins himself to the Lord is one spirit with Him."
1 Corinthians 6:17 See 1 Cor. 12:13).
(4) sealing (Eph. 1:13-14; 4:30).
"13 In Him, you also, after listening to the message of truth, the gospel of your salvation—having also believed, you were sealed in Him with the Holy Spirit of promise, 14 who is given as a pledge of our inheritance, with a view to the redemption of God's own

possession, to the praise of His glory."
Ephesians 1:13-14 "Do not grieve the
Holy Spirit of God, by whom you were
sealed for the day of redemption."
Ephesians 4:30

So, we are kept in, by, and for Jesus Christ,
and what a blessing to be kept by God, have a
spell, rejoice till you voice is hoarse! If you are
in Christ, you are eternally secure!

Kept every day from morn to night,
We know His promises are sure.
Kept by His truth, His power and might
No jot shall fail, while words endure.

Kept all the way from youth to age,
Thus far the Lord hath sheltered me.
Kept from the fangs of Satan's rage,
Safely we'll cross life's troubled sea.

Kept all these years by God's own hand,
To Him be praise and homage given.
Kept by His grace we'll hope to stand.
At evening time, in sight of Heaven.

Kept from the power of hell and sin.
Home of the pure in heart we'll see.
Kept by His love we'll here begin
The life that fills eternity.—Selected.

The Descriptive Greeting speaks revealing the *Prayer* for the believer

MacDonald, "The greeting is peculiarly suited to those who were facing the onslaught of those whose aim was to subvert their faith. Mercy means God's compassionate comfort and care for His beleaguered saints in times of conflict and stress. Peace is the serenity and confidence that comes from reliance on God's word and from looking above the circumstances for the accomplishment fo His own purposes. Love is the undeserved embrace of God for His dear people - a super-affection that should then be shared with others."

If we grow in God's mercy, peace, and love - we can literally face any and everything life throws at us!

THE MULTIPLICATION

May...multiplied - goes together!

The *Possibility*

It is an optative mood, "The mood used in prayers, wishes and other instances to denote verbal action that is possible." [Pocket Dictionary for the Study of New Testament

Greek]

The *Passivity*

It is in the passive voice, "The voice that conveys that the subject is being affected by or is the receiver of the verbal action." Pocket Dictionary for the Study of New Testament Greek.

The wish for *Plenty*

This verb, found in early Greek literature, has a basic meaning of "to be (or) become full." Depending upon the context, various shades of meaning occur: "to increase in number, multiply, abound, grow, spread." In Matthew 24:12 plēthunō [play-thoo-no] is used to indicate the extent and spread of lawlessness.

"Because lawlessness is increased, most people's love will grow cold." Matthew 24:12

In Acts, especially with reference to reports of the Church's progress, the idea is that of numerical growth as a result of the proclamation of the Word:

"The word of God kept on spreading; and the number of the disciples continued to increase greatly in Jerusalem, and a great many of the

priests were becoming obedient to the faith."
Acts 6:7

"So the church throughout all Judea and
Galilee and Samaria enjoyed peace, being built
up; and going on in the fear of the Lord and in
the comfort of the Holy Spirit, it continued to
increase." Acts 9:31

"But the word of the Lord continued to grow
and to be multiplied. Acts 12:24

There is a formula-use found in expressions of
strong wishes or desires, e.g., "May the grace
and peace of our Lord be yours in ever greater
measure" (cf. 1 Peter 1:2; 2 Peter 1:2; Jude
2).

Spurgeon writes, "The benediction of the
apostle is this, that this mercy, peace, and
love may be multiplied to you. Is not that a
beautiful word, "multiplied"?-not merely
increased, but multiplied. You know what it is
to increase; you add one to two, that is three;
but when you multiply, you say, "Three times
three, that is nine." Multiplying is a quick way
of growing. Oh, that you had all these
blessings multiplied, -that, if you have had
mercy, you might have ten times as much
mercy, -that, if you have had peace, you
might have a deeper, fuller, richer, more

abiding peace, multiplied peace, peace upon peace, "the peace of God, which passeth all understanding;"-and that, if you have had love, your love might be multiplied, squared, cubed! May the biggest figures that can be found multiply your love, for never did any man yet have too much love to God, or too much of the right kind of love to his fellow-men! May the Lord make us to grow in grace, to be filled with grace, to have these three graces multiplied unto us!"

THE MANIFESTATION
[What do we desire to be multiplied?]

Mercy

mercy - God in His mercy does not give us what we deserve. Instead, He gave our punishment to His own Son on the cross.

"Surely our griefs He Himself bore, And our sorrows He carried; Yet we ourselves esteemed Him stricken, Smitten of God, and afflicted." Isaiah 53:4

John MacArthur, "Whenever believers commit sin, they will always find an ample supply of mercy at God's throne of grace (Heb. 4:16). Paul told the Romans that God manifested "the riches of His glory upon vessels of mercy, which He prepared beforehand for glory" (Rom. 9:23). The "vessels of mercy," those sinners whom God has chosen for salvation, continually receive outpourings of His mercy, like cups or bowls that are constantly refilled with water."

"Mercy carries with it the Old Testament picture of God's loving-kindness or compassion. God's mercy helps believers day by day. Jude knew that the believers were facing difficult situations in the world—a society focused on selfish pleasure, ready to persecute believers at any provocation, with false teachers looking to tear the churches apart. Mercy helps believers in their times of need (Hebrews 4:16)." [Life Application New Testament Commentary]

Again, Charles Spurgeon, "Beloved, may you have mercy! You will always want it, for even a saint is a sinner still. May you have the mercy that will continue to forgive your sin, the mercy that will continue to wash your feet the mercies of providence that will supply your need, the mercies that will sustain you under trial, the mercies that will lead you on from strength to strength! May you have much mercy, for you will want it; and, blessed be God, "He delighteth in mercy."

Doctor Everett L. Worthington, Jr. is a professor of psychology at Virginia Commonwealth University and has won recognition on the subject of forgiveness. Dr. Worthington dedicated seven years of his life studying the physiological effects of forgiveness and its benefits. One day after mailing off his manuscript outlining a step-by-step process of forgiveness, his own ability was sorely tested when his mother was murdered. Doctor Worthington recalls: "On New Year's Eve, 1995, my mother was murdered. At first, I did not want to forgive the murderer. I wanted to beat his head in. Mercifully, though, I believe God gave me the grace to forgive the murder even though the murderer was never brought to justice. It was not easy to forgive such a brutal murder. A youth bludgeoned my mother to death with a crowbar during a botched burglary. If he had been caught and convicted, that would have made forgiving easier. Justice would have soaked up some of the bitter tears. As I look back on that event, from the perspective of years past, I have seen what I never saw during my first couple of years. I have marveled at God's mercy to me."

Peace

It speaks of peace, harmony, tranquility, health. From the day of the Fall man has been at war, with God. On the eve of the Millennium, Sir Cliff Richard lit the "eternal flame" atop a giant revolving globe in Birmingham, England's Centenary Square to promote world peace and harmony. Dubbed "The Flame of Hope" the flame was to symbolize world peace as the year 2000 began. Like the Olympic torch, it was meant to burn forever. But in 2004, the sponsors stopped paying its $12,000 annual natural gas bill. Birmingham's City Council balked at paying the bills; it also argued that the flame contributed to global warming and suggested substituting a flame-effect electric light. The West Bromwich Building Society finally agreed to help pay for the cost of the flame as part of a 12-month sponsorship deal with Birmingham City Council. Man lacks even the ability to keep symbols of peace going - they even fight over peace! What a contrast with Christ - He alone, as Prince of Peace brings eternal peace to the believer.

Love

Love - Spurgeon, "Jude next wishes that we may have love; that is to say, first, a sense of the love of God shed abroad in our heart by the Holy Ghost, a ravishing realization that God loves us with that everlasting love which knows no measure, nor change, nor end. May your heart dance at the very thought of the infinite love of God which he displays towards you! And then may you have love towards men, loving your neighbor as yourself with that compassionate love which is pictured in the parable of the Samaritan, that love which does not say, "Be ye warmed, and be ye filled," but which proves itself to be real by deeds of charity and acts of kindness! May you abound in love to God's people; may your love be exceeding abundant to those who are your brethren and sisters in Christ, whose names are written in the Lamb's book of life! I wish, dear friends, that you and I could be suffused with love. One said of Basil that he was a pillar of light; I would not so much care for that comparison as to be a pillar of love. Look at holy John; next to his Master, surely, and chiefly so because he abounded in love."

Few things more encouraging then realizing that God loves us!

Max Lucado wrote, "There are many reasons God saves you: to bring glory to Himself, to appease His justice, to demonstrate His sovereignty. But one of the sweetest reasons God saved you is because He is fond of you. He likes having you around. He thinks you are the best thing to come down the pike in quite a while... If God had a refrigerator, your picture would be on it. If He had a wallet, your photo would be in it. He sends you flowers every spring and a sunrise every morning. Whenever you want to talk, He'll listen. He can live anywhere in the universe, and He chose your heart. And the Christmas gift He sent you in Bethlehem? Face it, friend. He's crazy about you!"

S. Maxwell Coder summarizes:

"There is an upward look in the word mercy, an inward look in the word peace, and an outward look in the word love. These three related us properly to God, to our own inner being, and to our brethren around us. When they are multiplied, and only then, will we be able to cope with the great apostasy."

No matter what we are facing - we can face it
with God's mercy, peace, and love.
Living in a time torn with bitterness,
uncertainty and difficulty, which followed the
Civil War, John Greenleaf Whittier knew of one
resource in which he could put his trust—

Yet, in the maddening maze of things,
And tossed by storm and flood,
To one fixed trust my spirit clings;
I know that God is good!
I know not what the future hath
Of marvel or surprise,
Assured alone that life and death
His mercy underlies.
I know not where His islands lift
Their fronded palms in air;
I only know I cannot drift
Beyond His love and care.

—The Eternal Goodness

Chapter Two

A Defense of the Word of God

³ Beloved, while I was making every effort to write you about our common salvation, I felt the necessity to write to you appealing that you contend earnestly for the faith which was once for all handed down to the saints. ⁴ For certain persons have crept in unnoticed, those who were long beforehand marked out for this condemnation, ungodly persons who turn the grace of our God into licentiousness and deny our only Master and Lord, Jesus Christ. Jude 1:3-4

Paul wrote to Timothy, "Now you followed my teaching, conduct, purpose, faith, patience, love, perseverance," 2 Timothy 3:10

As one noted, "In the Greek text, the definite article precedes each of the descriptive nouns in verses 10 and 11, grammatically connecting each to the possessive pronoun my and thereby giving it repeated emphasis. The idea is, "But you followed my teaching, [my] conduct, [my] purpose, and so on. Every church, Christian college, Bible school, seminary, and other Christian organization should be led by and, in turn, reproduce leaders who not only are orthodox in doctrine and moral in lifestyle but also are courageous and committed defenders of the faith. They should be willing to follow the Lord and lead His church in dangerous times and circumstances and at any cost steadfastly hold up the banner of God's divine revelation in Scripture."

So, we have looked at the Descriptive Greeting, now we come to the Defense of the Word of God (Jude 3-4).

His *Desired Intention*

Beloved, while I was making every effort to write you about our common salvation - They were *Divinely* loved, or beloved. Jude sees how important it is for us to realize we are loved - vv.1, 2, 3, 12, 17, 20, 21. God designates Christ as "my beloved Son" (cf. Matt. 3:17; 12:18; 17:5; Mark 1:11; 9:7; Luke 3:22; 9:35; 2 Pet. 1:17). In 1 Cor. 4:17, Paul refers to Timothy as his "beloved son" since he was converted under the apostle's ministry. In Luke 20:13, agapētos refers to a person in the parable, though in reality it is applied to Christ as the Son of God. People are deemed "highly esteemed" or "beloved" in general contexts in Acts 15:25; Rom. 16:5 ff.; Eph. 5:1; 6:21; 1 Tim. 6:2. Rom. 1:7; 11:28 designates people as "beloved of God." The term "beloved" is also a form of address or greeting in Rom. 12:19; 1 Cor. 10:14; 2 Cor. 7:1; Phil. 2:12; Phlm. 2; Heb. 6:9; 1 Pet. 2:11; 2 Pet. 3:14 ff.; 1 John 4:1 ff.; Jude 3, 17, 20." [see, Expository Dictionary of Bible Words]

The fact that God has left us His love letter, the Bible, giving us a special message from Him every day, is in itself a great act of His love for us. A few years ago, the Harry S. Truman Library in Independence, MO made public 1,300 recently discovered letters that the late President wrote to his wife, Bess, over the course of a half-century. Mr. Truman had a lifelong rule of writing to his wife every day they were apart. He followed this rule whenever he was away on official business or whenever Bess left Washington to visit her beloved Independence. Scholars are examining the letters for any new light they may throw on political and diplomatic history. For our part, we were most impressed by the simple fact that every day he was away, the President of the United States took time out from his dealing with the world's most powerful leaders to sit down and write a letter to his wife.

The *Desired* intention

I was making every effort - the authors of the Bible did not just sit down and decide what to write! See, 2 Tim. 3:16-17. The words "Every effort," means "Haste, speed, zeal, effort, earnestness, diligence." Probably the best word would be eager, Jude was eager to write to them about their common salvation.

"Dear friends, although I was very eager to write to you about the salvation we share..." Jude 1:3 (NIV)

Like Jude we do well to follow God's leading, just because we desire to say or do something does not mean it is what we should say or do. While what we write is not under divine inspiration, we do have access to God's will and desires.

"12 So then, my beloved, just as you have always obeyed, not as in my presence only, but now much more in my absence, work out your salvation with fear and trembling; 13 for it is God who is at work in you, both to will and to work for His good pleasure." Philippians 2:12-13

"[Not in your own strength] for it is God Who is all the while effectually at work in you [energizing and creating in you the power and desire], both to will and to work for His good pleasure and satisfaction and delight."
Philippians 2:13 (AMP)

Do we follow God's desires - even when they are not ours? We must keep in mind that God know what is best and we don't.

Earl Weaver, former manager of the Baltimore Orioles had a rule that no one could steal a base unless given the steal sign. This upset Reggie Jackson because he felt he knew the pitchers and catchers well enough to judge who he could and could not steal off of. So one game he decided to steal without a sign. He got a good jump off the pitcher and easily beat the throw to second base. As he shook the dirt off his uniform, Jackson smiled with delight, feeling he had vindicated his judgment to his manager. Later Earl took Jackson aside and explained why he hadn't given the steal sign. "First, the next batter was Lee May, his best power hitter other than Jackson. When Jackson stole second, first base was left open, so the other team walked May intentionally, taking the bat out of his hands. Second, the following batter hadn't been strong against that pitcher, so Earl felt he had to send up a pinch hitter to try to drive in the men on base. That left Earl without bench strength later in the game when he needed it."The problem was, Jackson saw only his relationship to the pitcher and catcher. Weaver was watching the whole game. We, too, see only so far, but God sees the bigger picture. When he sends us a signal, it's wise to obey, no matter what we may think we know.

Their common *Deliverance*

common salvation - it means, salvation, deliverance, preservation. The noun is used 45 times. It has a wide range of meanings in the New Testament. In our context it has the meaning "personal salvation"—that is, the deliverance of the individual from bondage to sin."Not common as being of little importance, but common in the sense that it was for all— Jew and Gentile—for all people. Salvation is a deliverance from evil. In this instance it relates to a deliverance from the state of guilt and dominion of wrong-doing in this life, and includes the eternal deliverance in the world to come. All this is included in the gospel plan of salvation, and is offered to every son and daughter of the human race." [A Commentary and an Exposition of the Epistles of James, Peter, John and Jude]

"Simon Peter, a bond-servant and apostle of Jesus Christ, To those who have received a faith of the same kind as ours, by the righteousness of our God and Savior, Jesus Christ:" 2 Peter 1:1

McGee, "Common salvation." Let's understand that the word common is the English translation of the Greek word koines. The New Testament was not written in classical Greek but in koine Greek or common Greek, meaning that it was understood by everyone, educated and uneducated, all over the Roman Empire in the days of the apostles. When Jude said that he had intended to write of the "common salvation," he must have been referring to something that people throughout the Roman Empire would understand. Now Jude says here that he was planning on writing on some facet of our salvation. It could have been on redemption, on the person of Christ, on sanctification, or any number of themes, but he didn't write on any of those themes because "it was needful for me to write unto you, and exhort you that ye should earnestly contend for the faith which was once delivered unto the saints." The thought here is that the Holy Spirit detoured Jude from writing on some theme of the faith in order that he might sound a warning concerning the impending apostasy." [J. Vernon McGee's Thru the Bible]

What the church needed most was not a letter on salvation, as important as that is, but a letter on contending for the faith.

He yielded to *Divine Intervention*

I felt the necessity to write to you - "The presence of false teaching restrained him, impressing him with the urgent need to call the church to battle. His initial notion was to speak positively of the shared blessings of salvation. But that very salvation was under assault by apostates, hence his change of subjects. Like Paul, who wrote to the Corinthians, "For necessity is laid upon me; yes, woe is me if I do not preach the gospel" (1 Cor. 9:16), Jude felt the necessity—a heavy burden or mandate—to write. Agchō, the root of the noun rendered necessity, means literally "compress." Jude recognized that he was a watchman for the truth (cf. Ezek. 3:16-21) who could not simply watch in silence as his readers slipped into error." [MacArthur]

There is *Described clear Instruction*

The need to *Contend*

that you contend earnestly - This word means "to fight" or "to struggle" intensely. We get our word agonize from it. Here is some of the various translations:

"I fully intended, dear friends, to write to you about our common salvation, but I feel compelled to make my letter to you an earnest appeal to put up a real fight for the faith..." Jude 1:3 Phillips

"Dear friends, I've dropped everything to write you about this life of salvation that we have in common. I have to write insisting—begging!— that you fight with everything you have in you for this faith entrusted to us as a gift to guard and cherish." Jude 1:3 (MSG)

"The simple verb was used of athletes contending in the athletic contests. The word speaks of a vigorous, intense, determined struggle to defeat the opposition. Our word "agony" is the English spelling of the noun form of this word. The Greek athletes exerted themselves to the point of agony in an effort to win the contest. With such intense effort does Jude say that saints should defend the doctrines of Christianity." [Wuest's Word Studies - Wuest's Word Studies]

We must Battle for the Bible!

"Fight the good fight of faith; take hold of the eternal life to which you were called, and you made the good confession in the presence of many witnesses." 1 Timothy 6:12

"I have fought the good fight, I have finished the course, I have kept the faith;" 2 Timothy 4:7

W. A. Criswell, "A strong doctrinal preacher will build a strong church. A weak doctrinal preacher will build a weak church. It is the truth of doctrine that forms the backbone, the spine, the skeleton of the congregation. Without it the church is spineless, soft, flabby, formless, amorphous, without marching, converting, driving power. I would suppose that the one dominant characteristic that makes a jellyfish a jellyfish is that it has no spine, no backbone, no bone structure. Too many preachers and too many churches are like that. A woman came up to me recently and exclaimed: "Oh, we have formed the most wonderful church. It is perfect. It is delightful. My husband and I have just joined it and we are so happy in it. You do not have to believe anything to belong to our church. Anybody can join it." But I thought in my heart, what a conglomerate of nothing! True doctrine is the truth of God. The truth of God is found fully and marvelously revealed on the pages of the Holy Scriptures. Preach it! Do so fearlessly, courageously, powerfully, zealously, with deep conviction." [Criswell's Guidebook for Pastors]

The *Content* of what we are defending

for the faith - is the body of truths taught by the apostles.

"They were continually devoting themselves to the apostles' teaching and to fellowship, to the breaking of bread and to prayer." Acts 2:42

"But you, beloved, ought to remember the words that were spoken beforehand by the apostles of our Lord Jesus Christ," Jude 1:17

Morris, "The faith, is not in reference to the simple trust which we place in Christ in salvation, but to the entire body of Christian truth as revealed in the Holy Scriptures."

The Conclusion of that content

which was once for all handed down to the saints - that means there is a body of truth that is full and final!

McShane, "It would appear that by the time this epistle was written the apostolic doctrine had been fully established. The words "once for all" make this clear."

"Aren't you struck by that little phrase "once for all"? London's Rev. Dick Lucas, a faithful contender for the gospel, put the stunning reality behind these words this way: "[I]n Jude, the Christian faith is already in existence as a settled and final body of saving truths." Imagine! We are not free to change it, as if the faith were somehow still evolving and making its way in the world. According to Jude, "the faith" is not only full, but it already exists in final form. It is not subject to change!" [Preaching the Word - Preaching the Word – 1 & 2 Peter and Jude: Sharing Christ's Sufferings]

"Believers must fight with all their strength to preserve "the faith" which has been handed down to them. Hapax means "once for all," because the message of Christianity was given to the Church at the beginning; it had not come in installments. The content of the apostolic gospel is fixed, not to be revised for each new era." [Complete Biblical Library]

"They were to contend for the faith which was once delivered unto the saints. (Jude 1:3) The faith spoken of here is not the personal faith by which one is saved. Rather, it is the entire revelation from God; the whole body of truth as contained in His Word. Men and women down through the ages have attempted to add to and take away from the body of doctrine. This accounts for the great number of denominations and cults that are present today. This is why we stand so strongly on the Word of God as it was given to us. The Bible is our sole authority in all matters of faith and practice. The Bible contains the mind of God, the condition of man, and the clear, simple plan of salvation. The Lord Jesus Christ is the Wonderful and glorious theme of the Bible. His salvation shines forth from its pages as a guiding light to who desires to be saved. It is the source of truth and doctrine. Also, notice how the Holy Spirit led Jude to point out that this body of doctrine known as the faith was once delivered unto the saints. Not twice delivered. Not thrice delivered. It is not progressively being delivered. But it was once delivered! Those who claim that they are receiving revelations today are sadly mistaken. The Bible tells us that the revelation of God is complete and that no new revelation is being added. But when that which is perfect is come, then that which is in part shall be done away. (1 Corinthians 13:10) The body of truth, the faith as the Bible calls it, was finalized at a point of time in history. It was once delivered. God's word is both full and final." [Expository Pulpit Series]

"The faith" was the body of truth given once for all. In the Book of Acts it is called the apostles' doctrine: "And they continued steadfastly in the apostles' doctrine and fellowship, and in breaking of bread, and in prayers" (Acts 2:42). Notice that the apostles' doctrine is the first thing mentioned. Since that is number one on God's church parade, our church is not a church unless it is doing just that." [J. Vernon McGee's Thru the Bible]

John Philips, "The faith that has been "once delivered" does not refer to a creed or a formula of articles of belief. It refers instead to the substance of the complete New Testament teachings concerning the gospel and the church. That faith has been "delivered once for all," as the Revised Version puts it. It is the sum of the things that we must believe. It is something with which we must not tamper. We can reject categorically attempts to add to that "once for all" body of belief, as, for instance, the heretical Book of Mormon. The Mormons try to present that book as "another testament of Jesus Christ." It is nothing of the kind. It is part fiction, part forgery, and total delusion. "The faith... once delivered unto the saints" was neither defective nor deficient. It did not need the gradual addition over the centuries of Roman Catholic dogmas. Rome's dogmas and the doctrines of the New Testament are poles apart...The liberals, on the other hand, go to the opposite extreme. They do not want to add; they want to subtract. They see the chief doctrines of Christianity as repulsive and absurd and want to discard them in favor of humanism, psychology, and a blend of religious philosophies. So, before he deals with apostasy, Jude anchors the "beloved" to "the faith which was once delivered unto the saints..." [John Phillips Commentary Series]

Vincent, "Once (ἅπαξ) Not formerly, but once for all. So Rev., "No other faith will be given," says Bengel." [Word Studies in the New Testament]

Swindoll, "The faith" Jude admonishes us to contend for is the body of truth contained in the Scriptures...It was faith that was delivered "once for all."

MacDonald, "Notice that! Not "once upon a time" but once for all." The body of doctrine is complete. The canon is finished. Nothing more can be added. "If it's new it's not true, and if it's true it's not new." When some teacher claims to have a revelation which is above and beyond what is found in the Bible, we reject it out of hand. The faith has been delivered and we neither need nor heed anything else. This is our answer to the leaders of false cults with their books that claim equal authority with the Scriptures."

The last thing Paul wrote was 2 Timothy:

"16 All Scripture is given by inspiration of God, and is profitable for doctrine, for reproof, for correction, for instruction in righteousness, 17 that the man of God may be complete, thoroughly equipped for every good work."
2 Timothy 3:16-17

The last book in our Bible makes it clear:

"18 I testify to everyone who hears the words of the prophecy of this book: if anyone adds to them, God will add to him the plagues which are written in this book; 19 and if anyone takes away from the words of the book of this prophecy, God will take away his part from the tree of life and from the holy city, which are written in this book." Revelation 22:18-19

Bottom line is we are called upon to contend for, what we refer to today as the Bible, the written Word of God! We are not called to study other cultic books, we do not have to try and figure out whether some teacher's, so-called revelation, is from God - WE ARE CALLED UPON TO DEFEND GOD'S WRITTEN WORD! Such a defense is both needed and expected!

"But the Spirit explicitly says that in later times some will fall away from the faith, paying attention to deceitful spirits and doctrines of demons," 1 Timothy 4:1

People who create computer viruses disgust me! I got this off the internet, "Computer viruses are programs written by "mean" people. These virus programs are placed into a commonly used program so that program will run the attached virus program as it boots, therefore, it is said that the virus "infects" the executable file or program...Some viruses are programmed specifically to damage the data on your computer by corrupting programs, deleting files, or even erasing your entire hard drive. Many viruses do nothing more than display a message or make sounds, verbal comments at a certain time or a programming event after replicating themselves to be picked up by other users one way or another. Other viruses make your computer's system behave erratically or crash frequently..."

There are a variety of viruses:

OPRAH WINFREY VIRUS: Your 200MB hard drive suddenly shrinks to 80MB, and then slowly expands back to 200MB.

AT&T VIRUS: Every three minutes it tells you what great service you are getting.

ARNOLD SCHWARZENEGGER VIRUS: It keeps saying, "It'll be back."

GOVERNMENT ECONOMIST VIRUS: Nothing works, but all your diagnostic software says everything is fine.

GALLUP VIRUS: Sixty percent of the PCs infected will lose 38 percent of their data 14 percent of the time (plus or minus a 3.5 percent margin of error).

ADAM AND EVE VIRUS: Takes a couple of bytes out of your Apple.

MICHAEL JACKSON VIRUS: Hard to identify because it is constantly altering its appearance. This virus won't harm your PC, but it will trash your car.

PBS VIRUS: Your PC stops every few minutes to ask for money.

OLLIE NORTH VIRUS: Turns your printer into a document shredder.

JIMMY HOFFA VIRUS: Nobody can find it.

KEVORKIAN VIRUS: Helps your computer shut down whenever it wants to.

STAR TREK VIRUS: Invades your system in places where no virus has gone before.

HEALTH CARE VIRUS: Tests your system for a day, finds nothing wrong, and sends you a bill for $4,500.

OBAMA VIRUS: Your computer refuses to listen to you, it becomes bigger and bigger until it just takes over your computer.

False teachers are disgusting viruses that would like to ruin any and every church! Think of your computer as the Bible - viruses seek to distort or destroy it. But there is anti-virus programs - thanks to one former member, I have Norton Internet Security. It is constantly stopping viruses from tearing up my computer. Christ is to be like that - a Bible Security system! We are to know the Word of God, share it, and firmly and aggressively stand against those who would either add or take away from! Every year, thousands upon thousands of wildebeests run a sort of marathon. The African Savannah dries up for weeks. Then, rains come to the north.

Small herds of wildebeests join other herds of the hog-like creatures as they run for days. Covering many miles at a thundering speed, the larger herds grow to an unbelievable two million. Driven by instinct, the wildebeest perform their yearly ritual, running at full speed. Then, all at once, they come to an orchestrated stop. There, at the edge of a particular river, they sense danger in the air. Baboons in the trees overhead watch with great anticipation, knowing what is going to happen next.

A few wildebeests venture to the edge of the river. The water is so inviting after the dry season and after their long, long journey. Oh, to take from the cool water. The feeling of danger is intense, but so is their desire for the refreshing water. The few wildebeests that ignore their feelings of danger and begin to drink are at once taken in by the cool refreshing river water. Then, in one swift action, large hungry crocodiles emerge from beneath the river. They grab their victims in their powerful jaws and yank them into the water. The wildebeests are torn limb from limb! What had briefly seemed a refreshing source of life-giving water quickly turned into a deceptive death-trap. We must Defend the Word of God, because if we depart from the Scriptures, we will be taken in by the tricks of false teachers. We must test all teaching and preaching by the Word of God!

Let's review, we have seen his Desired Intention; and the Divine Intervention; and the Directions of clear Instruction. Now we come to the fact that they needed to defend the Word because of a Definite Invasion.

A Definite Invasion

By Deceptive People

For certain persons have crept in unnoticed - These Men, certain persons, are false teachers. No doubt there was a leader among them; false teachers always have a ringleader. A classic example of such false teaching in our day is Scientology, and they have a promoter as well. In 1954, science fiction writer L. Ron Hubbard founded the religion Scientology. It is a religion without a God. It teaches inter-galactic travel, reincarnation, and mind control among other strange ideas the science fiction writer taught. When Hubbard died in 1986, he told his believers he would make himself visible within 13 years of his death at a California desert mansion. One of the most powerful leaders of Scientology who emerged after Hubbard's death was David Miscavige. Miscavige recruited actor Tom Cruise into the cult and through the years immersed Cruise into the strange teachings. The religion has grown to more than 10 million world-wide, enlisting other celebrities such as John Travolta, Kirstie Alley, Jenna Elfman and Chick Correa. But it is Cruise who has had the greatest impact in recruiting others. Across 90 nations, 5,000 people hear his word of Scientology—every hour, International

Scientology News proclaimed last year. Every minute of every hour someone reaches for L. Ron Hubbard technology... simply because they know Tom Cruise is a Scientologist."

Their *Manner* - have crept in unnoticed

"For certain men have crept in stealthily [gaining entrance secretly by a side door]..." Jude 1:4 (AMP)

"I say this because some godless teachers have wormed their way in among you..." Jude 1:4 (TLB)

"What has happened is that some people have infiltrated our ranks..." Jude 1:4 (MSG)

"In classical Greek literature, the word referred to slipping poison into someone's glass. [Liddell and Scott, A Greek-English Lexicon]. As poison dropped furtively into a silver chalice, these men surreptitiously penetrated the church. And their effect was lethal, striking at the very core of Christian truth."

While the cults always have a main leader, they do not do most of the dirty work.

It is their followers who are trained to infiltrate churches. Of course they are not limited to the local church. "In today's church, such apostasy takes many forms. False teachers write books and edit publications, speak on radio and television, teach in colleges and seminaries, preach from pulpits, and have Web sites on the Internet."

""Be on guard for yourselves and for all the flock, among which the Holy Spirit has made you overseers, to shepherd the church of God which He purchased with His own blood." Acts 20:28

"But it was because of the false brethren secretly brought in, who had sneaked in to spy out our liberty which we have in Christ Jesus, in order to bring us into bondage." Galatians 2:4

"But false prophets also arose among the people, just as there will also be false teachers among you, who will secretly introduce destructive heresies, even denying the Master who bought them, bringing swift destruction upon themselves." 2 Peter 2:1

"The phrase *crept in unawares* means to "settle in alongside... to enter secretly, slip in stealthily." These apostates secretly slip in and settle down in the Church with their wicked intentions known only to themselves. They come to Church, sit in the worship services and Sunday-school classes, attend the Church fellowships, etc. They are part of the everyday life of the Church except for one important thing—they are imposters. They are not present for the good of the Church, but for the destruction of it. An apostate is a sneaky crook who has no honor. Just like a robber will not call you up and confess that he is going to rob your house at such and such a time, an apostate will not announce his evil reason for being present in the congregation. Oh no! He is much too smart for that. His intention is to go as long as possible unnoticed while all along doing his wicked work. There are almost always tares among the wheat. Someone has well said, "Wherever God sets up a house of prayer, the devil always builds a chapel" [Expository Pulpit Series]

False teachers are not what they appear to be! They often look good but they are sheep in wolves clothing. Reminds me of A MAN driving down a dirt road when he noticed an unusual pig. The pig had a little limp when he walked. When he got a little closer, he noticed the pig had an artificial leg. He had never seen anything like that, so he pulled in the drive to ask the pig farmer about it. He said to the farmer, "I have never, ever seen an artificial limb on an animal in general, and especially on a pig." "Well," said the farmer, "let me tell you about that pig. One day, my little granddaughter was walking out in front of the tractor. The tractor was going to mow her down, but the pig jumped in and knocked her out of the way. On another occasion, my grandson was drowning, and the pig jumped into the water and saved him... I just didn't have the heart to eat the pig all at once." The false teacher is like that - they often come across as kind and loving but they are not! We must Defend the Word of God because of Deceptive false teachers that seek to distort and destroy sound doctrine.

In the mid-1950's there was a popular American television program called "To Tell the Truth." Three guests on the show would claim to be the same person. Four panelists would then ask the guests questions to determine who was telling the truth. After a set time was up, each panelist voted for his or her choice as to who was telling the truth. Then the host of the show asked, "Will the real... [John Doe or whoever] please stand up?" In many ways, this game is being played out in churches throughout the world. People are presenting themselves or claiming to be godly. Is there a sure way to know who is telling the truth? You bet! Check them out according to God's written Word.

Their Damnation is Predicted

those who were long beforehand marked out for this condemnation - Their condemnation predicted long ago in the Old Testament. Phillips, "The word for "before ordained" means literally "to write before." In other words, the judgment that awaits the apostates has been stated of old. Jude's whole thesis, with his many appeals to the Old Testament, substantiates that position. One translator suggests the rendering "who have been written up beforehand," referring to the ancient custom of posting ahead of time the names of defendants who are scheduled to appear before the court for trial. The term of old is not applied here to God's eternal purposes. It points to prophecies given of old."

"19 When they say to you, "Consult the mediums and the spiritists who whisper and mutter," should not a people consult their God? Should they consult the dead on behalf of the living? 20 To the law and to the testimony! If they do not speak according to this word, it is because they have no dawn [light]. 21 They will pass through the land hard-pressed and famished, and it will turn out that when they are hungry, they will be enraged and curse their king and their God as they face upward. 22 Then they will look to the earth, and behold, distress and darkness, the gloom of anguish; and they will be driven away into darkness." Isaiah 8:19-22

"13 "The prophets are as wind, And the word is not in them. Thus it will be done to them!" 14 Therefore, thus says the LORD, the God of hosts, "Because you have spoken this word, Behold, I am making My words in your mouth fire And this people wood, and it will consume them. Jeremiah 5:13-14

And the New Testament predict their terrifying end!

"5 Do you not remember that while I was still with you, I was telling you these things? 6 And you know what restrains him now, so that in his time he will be revealed. 7 For the mystery of lawlessness is already at work; only he who now restrains will do so until he is taken out of the way. 8 Then that lawless one will be revealed whom the Lord will slay with the breath of His mouth and bring to an end by the appearance of His coming; 9 that is, the one whose coming is in accord with the activity of Satan, with all power and signs and false wonders, 10 and with all the deception of wickedness for those who perish, because they did not receive the love of the truth so as to be saved." 2 Thessalonians 2:5-10

"1 But false prophets also arose among the people, just as there will also be false teachers among you, who will secretly introduce destructive heresies, even denying the Master who bought them, bringing swift destruction upon themselves. 2 Many will follow their sensuality, and because of them the way of the truth will be maligned; 3 and in their greed they will exploit you with false words; their judgment from long ago is not idle, and their destruction is not asleep." 2 Peter 2:1-3

Perhaps you've seen the movie the Green Mile, those on death row walk the green mile to face sure death in the electric chair. As they walk the repeated phrase "dead man walking" can be heard. These false teachers are dead men walking! The truth is there is only one way to meet this Deception and that is with true Doctrine. As one noted, "With the wave of false prophets and false teachings that are rising in our time, it's important that we know and understand the truth of Scripture. With the ever increasing number of false teachings, we should be studying the Word so that we can remain firmly planted and keep from being swayed. Paul tells us in 2 Timothy 2:15 to "Study to show yourself approved unto God, a workman that needs not to be ashamed, rightly dividing the word of truth (KJV)." We are also told to "give attention to reading, to exhortation, [and] to doctrine" in 1 Timothy 4:13. Not only that, but we are even warned in Jude 3-4 that we need to "contend earnestly for the faith" because of these false teachers creeping in; in other words, we are commanded to fight for the truth of Scripture, which can only be done by being prepared and studying the Word. It's important to understand that the only way we're going to be able to know the truth of Scripture is to be engulfed in the studying of it. There's no way in the world that we, as Christians, are going to be able to testify against false teachings unless we know the Word for ourselves and know how to interpret it. At the same time, we should be able to follow up in the Scriptures after hearing our pastors preach in order to make sure that everything they have said lines up with what is written (Acts 17:11). There is no reason that today's Christians should be lemmings who mindlessly follow after anything that sounds good; we should all be well versed in the biblical texts and know how to exegete (interpret) Scripture. We have to be wary of having itching ears and allowing ourselves to fall prey to false teaching just because it sounds good or makes us feel better about ourselves, like many today are doing (2 Timothy 4:3). Just so we're on the same page, this does not mean that you have to go to seminary or Bible college; it simply means learning how to study the Word of God and how to use a Bible dictionary and commentary so that you can correctly interpret the texts." [Read, Pray, Worship, Live.: Teaching the Fundamentals]

Their *Doctrine is Perverted*

They are *Destitute* of a reverence for God

ungodly persons - "These men are called ungodly. The word is asebēs, "destitute of reverential awe toward God, impious."

Vines, "Original Word: ἀσέβεια, asebeia [as-eb-ace] Usage Notes: "impiety, ungodliness," is used of (a) general impiety, Rom. 1:18; Rom. 11:26; 2 Tim. 2:16; Titus 2:12; (b) "ungodly" deeds, Jude 1:15, "to execute judgment upon all, and to convict all the ungodly of all their ungodly deeds which they have done in an ungodly way, and of all the harsh things which ungodly sinners have spoken against Him." Jude 1:15 (c) of lusts or desires after evil things, Jude 1:18, "that they were saying to you, "In the last time there will

be mockers, following after their own ungodly lusts." Jude 1:18 It is the opposite of eusebeia, "godliness." Note: Anomia is disregard for, or defiance of, God's laws; asebeia is the same attitude towards God's Person...Adjective...Usage Notes: "impious, ungodly" (akin to A), "without reverence for God," not merely irreligious, but acting in contravention of God's demands:
"8 But we know that the Law is good, if one uses it lawfully, 9 realizing the fact that law is not made for a righteous person, but for those who are lawless and rebellious, for the ungodly and sinners, for the unholy and profane, for those who kill their fathers or mothers, for murderers" 1 Timothy 1:8-9
"15 to execute judgment upon all, and to convict all the ungodly of all their ungodly deeds which they have done in an ungodly way, and of all the harsh things which ungodly sinners have spoken against Him." 16 These are grumblers, finding fault, following after their own lusts; they speak arrogantly, flattering people for the sake of gaining an advantage." Jude 1:15-16 [Vine's Expository Dictionary of Old Testament and New Testament Words]

"For certain men have crept in stealthily [gaining entrance secretly by a side door]. Their doom was predicted long ago, ungodly (impious, profane) persons..." Jude 1:4 (AMP)

"...They have no real reverence for God..."
Jude 1:3 (Phillips NT)

"This word has the same meaning in every place where it is used. The prefix "un" means to be without. Joined to the word "godly," it means that the person, the nation or the subject under consideration is without God. The ungodly person may be beautiful in character, attractive in manner, cultivated, refined and educated, but he is living without God. He has no faith in God, and may be rebellious toward God. He may be quite religious in his outward actions, and yet have no knowledge personally of Jesus Christ. Such a person is un-godly." [A Dictionary of Bible Types]

They *Distort* Grace

who turn the grace of our God into licentiousness - CBL, "In the New Testament aselgeia is joined with the most heinous of sins such as covetousness, adultery, lewdness, and drunkenness."

Barclay characterizes aselgeia as "shameless greediness," "bestial pleasure," and "pure self-enjoyment," and he says that it is "in many

ways the ugliest word in the list of New
Testament sins" [New Testament Words,
pp.60, 61].

See Mark 7:22; Romans 13:13; 2 Peter 2:2,
7, 18.).

Basil characterizes this sin as a "condition of
the soul which does not know and cannot
endure the torment which discipline makes for
it."

Lightfoot says that "a man can be unclean,
and hide his sin; he does not become aselgēs
until he shocks public decency" (Epistle of St.
Paul to the Galatians, p.210).

This touches the very essence of sin. Josephus
combined aselgeia with mania, "madness." He
said that aselgeia was the sin of Jezebel
(Antiquities 8.13.1). Those under the control
of this sin do not care what others say or
think, as long as they can satisfy their desires.
Conscience is strangled and shame is "put to
flight" in the heart of the one who commits
aselgeia. It is said that the inhabitants of
Sodom spoke openly of their sin (Isaiah 3:9).
Thus aselgeia denotes open licentiousness and
shameless sin." "(especially of a person or
their behaviour) sexual in an uncontrolled and

socially unacceptable way" [Cambridge Dictionary]

It is a total lack of moral restraint! A lack of control, a blatant disregard and rejection of God's Word.

"Let us behave properly as in the day, not in carousing and drunkenness, not in sexual promiscuity and sensuality, not in strife and jealousy." Romans 13:13

"and they, having become callous, have given themselves over to sensuality for the practice of every kind of impurity with greediness." Ephesians 4:19

Reminds me of the "The rock festival" that was held in the heartland of Midwest America, Labor Day weekend, 1970. Between 20,000 and 25,000 came to a wheat field near Pittsburg, Kansas. They came in a state of unconventional dress and birthday clothes to attend what was billed as a rock musical festival but it turned out to be a wild orgy of promiscuous sex and narcotics. They were not a bunch of innocent youth, but rather the worst elements of society. Among them were hard-core revolutionaries. The American flag was desecrated. They waded and wallowed in filth. The sale and use of narcotics were wide open. It was the biggest pot party and sex orgy the Midwest has ever seen. There was display of nudity, and there were mixed nude swimming parties in a nearby creek. With no sanitation facilities and failure to comply with health regulations, one can imagine what the place was like. The former Kansas Governor and Presidential candidate, Alf Landon said: "They call these things festivals, but I have another name for them—'feasts of hell.'

"No matter what the false teaching is, it will enslave. The false teacher who denies Christ and God's Word removes the supreme authority over man's life. Therefore, man is basically free to live in selfishness and greed, desire and lust. He is left to seek as much pleasure and as many possessions as he desires upon earth. But in the end, man discovers something. The more he gets, the more he wants. It may be comfort, money, sex, position, or authority; it does not matter. Man's nature is such that he wants more and more. Man must be restrained by an authority above himself, that is, by God and by God's Word. If he is not, then he becomes enslaved to his passions and to the corruption of the world. This is one of the terrible fallacies of all false teachings. They all enslave man to this world: not a single false teaching can usher a man through the door of death into eternal life. Only Jesus Christ can do that. Note the clear truth: whatever overcomes a man, that very thing enslaves him." [Practical Word Studies in the New Testament]

Apparently all this is done under the guise of God's grace! But grace never encourages anyone to sin!

"1 What shall we say then? Are we to continue in sin so that grace may increase? 2 May it never be! How shall we who died to sin still live in it?" Romans 6:1-2

"For you were called to freedom, brethren; only do not turn your freedom into an opportunity for the flesh, but through love serve one another." Galatians 5:13

"11 For the grace of God has appeared, bringing salvation to all men, 12 instructing us to deny ungodliness and worldly desires and to live sensibly, righteously and godly in the present age," Titus 2:11-12

D. A. Carson, a professor at Trinity Evangelical Divinity School, used to meet with a young man from French West Africa for the purpose of practicing their German. He writes:

"Once a week or so, we had had enough, so we went out for a meal together and retreated

to French, a language we both knew well. In the course of those meals we got to know each other. I learned that his wife was in London, training to be a medical doctor. He was an engineer who needed fluency in German in order to pursue doctoral studies in engineering in Germany. I soon discovered that once or twice a week he disappeared into the red-light district of town. Obviously he went to pay his money and have his woman. Eventually I got to know him well enough that I asked him what he would do if he discovered that his wife was doing something similar in London. "Oh," he said, "I'd kill her."
"That's a bit of a double standard, isn't it?" I asked. "You don't understand. Where I come from in Africa, the husband has the right to sleep with many women, but if a wife is unfaithful to her husband she must be killed."
"But you told me you were raised in a mission school. You know that the God of the Bible does not have double standards like that." He gave me a bright smile and replied, "Ah, le bon Dieu, il doit nous pardonner; c'est son metier [Ah, God is good. He's bound to forgive us; that's his job]."

That's what I call an abuse of grace! Yes, we all sin on a daily basis and need to confess and forsake sin but that does not mean we treat sin lightly or take God's grace for granted.

They *Deny* the Son of God

and deny our only Master and Lord, Jesus Christ - This is a very strong Greek term; in fact, we derive our English word despot from it. It can be used of human masters but it also used of God as Master. Note Acts 4:24:

"When they heard this, they raised their voices together in prayer to God. "Sovereign Lord," they said, "you made the heaven and the earth and the sea, and everything in them." Acts 4:24 (NIV)

The Da Vinci Code is one modern example of denying the proper place that the Lord Jesus should be given. Here is a lengthy quote worth quoting:

"The line between entertainment and education is slim these days. The Da Vinci Code is fictional entertainment that is subtly educating people today to deny the divinity of Christ and to call into question the entire Christian faith. Thus far, about 60.5 million copies of the book are in print, rendering it read by one hundred million people, according to an ABC report. Large percentages of people in Europe, America, and Canada are putting faith in the stories. Movie gross sales are over two hundred fifty million dollars. Dan Brown's book is based on a book written in 1982 titled The Holy Blood and the Holy Grail. Some Christians say it's no big deal; it's just a novel. But it is a big deal when people confuse fiction with fact and lose their faith. We are told to "contend for the faith that was once for all entrusted to the saints" (Jude 3). To this end I deliver this message on The Da Vinci Code deception for a renewal of faith.

The story line goes like this: Jesus was human, not divine. He was married to Mary Magdalene, who was pregnant at the Crucifixion. Jesus intended for her to lead the church, but the male-dominated apostolic band wanted Peter to lead. So Mary fled under protection to France and gave birth to their daughter, Sarah, after Jesus' death.

The royal line of Jesus still exists in France and is protected by a sacred order called the Priory of Sion, whose military arm was the Knights Templar. Mary Magdalene is the actual Holy Grail at the Last Supper, not a chalice used in the Passover, and her remains are in a sarcophagus hidden in France. A sect of the Catholic Church called Opus Dei has sought for centuries to destroy the heirs of Christ. All of this was done to subjugate women to a place of submission and to further the political power of the church. Opus Dei will do anything necessary to keep a lid on the secret of Jesus and Mary. Leonardo Da Vinci, Sir Isaac Newton, Victor Hugo, and other influential persons were members of the Priory of Sion. Da Vinci hid the secret in The Last Supper. Supposedly, John to the right of Jesus is not John at all but Mary Magdalene. (In reality, however, the drawings on Da Vinci's sketches of the fresco have the names of the disciples written underneath the figures clearly showing John, not Mary, at Jesus' side.). The real story of Mary was concealed in hidden codes and symbols. The remains of Mary Magdalene are revealed as being located under the floor of the Louvre in Paris. In the movie, Sir Leigh Teabing, a secret member of Opus Dei, says to Dr. Robert Langdon (played by Tom Hanks), a symbologist from Harvard, "If it were proved that Jesus was not divine, but merely a man, it would shake the very foundations of Christianity."

This statement is true. Seventy-eight percent of Americans confess to be Christians ("Mixing Fun and Faith," Reader's Digest, June, 2006, 32). Christianity is the largest religion in the world, with over one-third of the world's population claiming to be Christian. That's a whole lot of shakin' going on if The Da Vinci Code is true and Jesus is not divine!

The foundation of our faith is the divinity of Christ. Who is Jesus? This is the question many religions struggle with. Judaism recognizes Jesus as a prophet, but not as the Son of God. Islam derives its information on Jesus from the New Testament, although it changes it by presenting Him only as a prophet. It claims that Jesus did not die but a substitute took His place because God would never allow His prophet to be crucified. They believe God took Him to heaven and will send Him back in the last days to judge the world—a legend also found in the Gnostic Gospels.

As Jesus approached the Cross, He wanted to make sure the disciples really knew Him. So He asked them, "Who do people say the Son of Man is?" (Matt. 16:13). After they gave Him several answers, He asked the most important question He ever asked: "Who do you say I am?" (v. 15). Peter replied on behalf of them all: "You are the Christ, the Son of the living God" (v. 16). Jesus then replied, "On this rock I will build my church" (v. 18). The "rock" was not Peter but the revelation of who Jesus is. Remember these hymn lyrics:

"On Christ, the solid Rock, I stand;
All other ground is sinking sand."

The Da Vinci Code states that the early disciples did not believe in the divinity of Jesus and that the concept of Jesus' full divinity was invented by the Roman emperor Constantine at the Council of Nicaea in AD 325. The council convened under the leadership of Constantine in an effort to unify the church on this issue. Division in the church, he thought, could split his empire. Arius taught that Jesus was not fully God because He had a beginning in God and, therefore, was not eternal. His movement was called Arianism. After Eusebius, bishop of Caesarea, presented Arius' position, it was overwhelmingly rejected by the council. The book claims that it was a narrow vote, when actually only two of the three-hundred-plus bishops present refused to sign the Nicene Creed. The first Nicene Creed stated that Christ is "true God of true God."

The Da Vinci Code suggests that Constantine only chose the Gospels of Matthew, Mark, Luke, and John because they fit his agenda of male power. Actually, Justin Martyr, who was martyred in AD 165, argued for only four gospels. The claim that eighty other gospels were rejected by the council because they taught that Jesus wanted Mary Magdalene to be the leader of the church is false. The council never considered the issue of the canon of New Testament books.

The Da Vinci Code also states that ancient Israel worshiped both the male Jehovah and the female counterpart, the Shekinah, and that centuries later the church suppressed goddess worship and eliminated the divine feminine. This, of course, is bogus.

People might ask, "What difference does it make if Jesus is divine or not? He was a good man who made the world a better place and gave us the greatest teachings on love." It makes all the difference. If Jesus is not divine, then He is just like us, He cannot save us, His death has no redemptive power, and He has not been raised from the dead. "And if Christ has not been raised," Paul tells us clearly, "our preaching is useless and so is your faith. More than that, we are then found to be false witnesses about God, for we have testified about God that he raised Christ from the dead.... If Christ has not been raised, your faith is futile; you are still in your sins. Then those also who have fallen asleep in Christ are lost. If only for this life we have hope in Christ, we are to be pitied more than all men. But Christ has indeed been raised from the dead" (1 Cor. 15:14-20, emphasis added). The key is the New Testament; these books are the works of the eyewitnesses of Jesus. Every New Testament book states clearly the divinity of Jesus as the Son of God, sinless, who came to redeem us from the law of sin and death.

- In the Gospels Jesus is called "the Son of God" forty-nine times, "the only begotten Son" five times, "my Son" ten times, "the Son" thirty-four times, "his Son" twenty-four times, and "the

Son of Man" (a messianic title) eighty-six times.

- What did the prophets say about the Messiah? They revealed His lordship, oneness with the Father, and eternalness (Ps. 110:1; Isa. 7:14; 9:6-7; Mic. 5:2).
- What did Jesus say about Himself? Jesus was controversial because He made Himself equal with God. In John 10:33 we find evidence that Jesus claimed to be God, and in verse 36 He said, "I am God's Son." To the disciples He said, "Anyone who has seen me has seen the Father" (14:9). When Buddha was teaching on enlightenment, people asked him what he was, not who he was: "Are you a god?... An angel?... A saint?" Buddha replied, "No." Then people asked, "Then what are you?" Buddha answered, "I am awake." This is a famous anecdotal story in Buddhism. But the question to Jesus is not "What are you?" but "Who are you?"
  During the Passion Week we read: While the Pharisees were gathered together, Jesus asked them, "What do you think about the Christ? Whose son is he?" "The son of David," they

replied. He said to them, "How is it then that David, speaking by the Spirit, calls him 'Lord'? For he says, 'The Lord said to my Lord: "Sit at my right hand until I put your enemies under your feet."' If then David calls him 'Lord,' how can he be his son?" No one could say a word in reply, and from that day on no one dared to ask him any more questions (Matt. 22:41-46).

- What did God the Father say about Jesus? The voice of God came from heaven at Jesus' baptism: "This is my Son, whom I love; with him I am well pleased" (3:17). Again, at the Mount of Transfiguration, God spoke to Peter, James, and John: "This is my Son, whom I love; with him I am well pleased. Listen to him!" (17:5).
- What did the angels say about Jesus? Before Jesus' birth an angel spoke with Mary: "You will be with child and give birth to a son, and you are to give him the name Jesus. He will be great and will be called the Son of the Most High.... His kingdom will never end." "How will this be," Mary asked the angel, "since I am a virgin?" The angel answered, "The Holy Spirit will come

upon you, and the power of the Most High will overshadow you. So the holy one to be born will be called the Son of God" (Luke 1:30-35). To the shepherds in the fields of Bethlehem, an angel said, "Do not be afraid. I bring you good news of great joy that will be for all the people. Today in the town of David a Savior has been born to you; he is Christ the Lord" (2:10-11).

- What did the demons say about Jesus? Mark's Gospel tells of Jesus being thronged by crowds wanting to be healed: "Whenever the evil spirits saw him, they fell down before him and cried out, 'You are the Son of God'" (3:11). When Jesus met the demoniac of Gadara and rebuked the demons in him, the man fell on his knees and shouted at the top of his voice, "What do you want with me, Jesus, Son of the Most High God?" (5:7).

- What did the disciples say about Jesus? When Jesus asked Martha of Bethany if she believed that He was the resurrection and the life, she replied, "Yes, Lord... I believe that you are the Christ, the Son of God, who was to come into the world" (John 11:27).

- And what of Mary Magdalene? She was the first one to see Jesus in the garden of the empty tomb, along with the "the other Mary" (the wife of Clopas; Matt. 27:56; John 19:25): "They came to him, clasped his feet and worshiped him" (Matt. 28:9). Jesus said to her, "'Do not hold on to me, for I have not yet returned to the Father. Go instead to my brothers and tell them, "I am returning to my Father and your Father, to my God and your God.'" Mary Magdalene went to the disciples with the news: 'I have seen the Lord!' And she told them that he had said these things to her" (John 20:17-18).
- When Thomas met the risen Lord, Jesus told him to put his hand in the scars and "stop doubting and believe" (v. 27). Thomas declared in praise, "My Lord and My God!" (v. 28).
- John writes: "In the beginning was the Word, and the Word was with God, and the Word was God.... The Word became flesh and made his dwelling among us. We have seen his glory, the glory of the One and Only, who came

from the Father, full of grace and truth" (1:1-4, 14).

- Peter proclaimed, "Salvation is found in no one else, for there is no other name under heaven given to men by which we must be saved" (Acts 4:12). Peter calls Christ "a lamb without blemish or defect... chosen before the creation of the world... revealed in these last times for your sake" (1 Peter 1:18-20).
- Stephen, the first martyr of the faith, when dying, looked up to heaven and said, "I see heaven open and the Son of Man standing at the right hand of God." He prayed, "Lord Jesus, receive my spirit" and cried out, "Lord, do not hold this sin against them" (Acts 7:55-61).
- Paul says of Jesus, "Who being in very nature God, did not consider equality with God something to be grasped...Therefore God exalted him to the highest place and gave him the name that is above every name, that at the name of Jesus every knee should bow... and every tongue confess that Jesus Christ is Lord" (Phil. 2:6-11).

In Colossians he says, "He is the image

of the invisible God...All things were created by him and for him" (1:15-20).

- Hebrews says, "The Son is the radiance of God's glory" (1:1-3).
- The Revelator says of his vision of Christ: "When I saw him, I fell at his feet as though dead. Then he placed his right hand on me and said: 'Do not be afraid. I am the First and the Last. I am the Living One; I was dead, and behold I am alive forever and ever! And I hold the keys of death and Hades'" (Rev. 1:17-18). At the end of the age he sees Christ returning as King of kings (19:11-16).
- What did the early church fathers say about Jesus? The early church fathers confirmed what the New Testament says. In a letter to the Ephesians, Ignatius of Antioch refers to Jesus as "God existing in flesh."
Polycarp of Smyrna, a student of John the apostle, sent a letter to the church at Philippi between AD 112 and AD 118. In it he speaks of the divinity of Jesus and His exaltation to heaven. He was martyred around AD 160.
Justin Martyr, who grew up in Israel, was impressed by the steadfast faith of Christians who died for their faith. He became a Christian and leader of the

church. He wrote, "If you had understood what has been written by the prophets, you would not have denied that [Jesus] was God." He was martyred in AD 165.

Irenaeus became bishop of Lyons in AD 177. He battled Gnosticism and wrote in his commentary on John 1:1, "All distinctions between the Father and Son vanish, for the one God made all things through His word."

One hundred years before Constantine, Tertullian (c. AD 155-c. AD 220) taught that Christ was fully divine and fully human [Erwin W. Lutzer, The Da Vinci Deception, Wheaton, IL: Tyndale House, 2004].

C. S. Lewis, in Mere Christianity, said there is only one of three possibilities about a man who claims to be God: either he is a lunatic, a liar, or Lord. As man, Jesus was born in Bethlehem's manger; but as God, He is from everlasting to everlasting. As man, He spoke in parables; but as God, He spoke the world into being. As man, He walked the streets of Jerusalem and Capernaum; but as God, He walked on the water. As man, He was hungry; but as God, He said, "I am the bread of life." As man, He was thirsty; but as God, He said, "I give you living water." As man, He was tired; but as God, He said, "I will give you rest." As man, He was tempted; but as God, He knew no sin. As man, He prayed; but as God, He answered prayer. As man, He was nailed to a cross; but as God, He arose on the third day as Lord! The entire New Testament was written for one reason: "Jesus did many other miraculous signs in the presence of his disciples, which are not recorded in this book. But these are written that you may believe that Jesus is the Christ, the Son of God, and that by believing you may have life in his name" (John 20:30-31).

Here's the bottom line: Jesus claimed to be the Son of God, divine, sinless, the sacrifice for our sins, and the only way to salvation. You must be born again through faith in Him (John 3:16; 1 John 5:1-12).

At the end of the movie, Robert Langdon helps Sophie Neveu, a young cytologist, realize that she is the only living heir of Jesus Christ. He asks her, "What would the heir of Christ do? Reveal the truth, that Jesus was not divine, and destroy faith, or renew their faith?" This question strikes at the point of the novel—that faith is based on fiction, not historical fact. However, our faith is not based on fiction but fact—Jesus is the way, the truth, and the life. Thomas Aquinas expounded on Jesus' claim:

"I am the Way, the Truth, and the Life. Without the Way, no journey can be taken. Without the Truth, no truth can be known. Without the Life, no life can be lived. I am the Way which must be followed; I am the Truth which must be believed; I am the Life for which man must hope." The call of Christ is to believe in Him. What does that mean? Acknowledge Christ as the Son of God. Believe in Him. Trust Him to save you and forgive you of your sins. Commit yourself to Him and follow Him as Lord of your life." Defending the Word of God is most needed in a society that has created its own belief system - we must stand on and lift up the truth as found in God's Word. John Wesley's reply to the statement, "I never will again be united with any who will not let others choose their own religion" was "Then you will never unite with any but knaves; for no honest men who preside over any community will let the members of it do what they judge to be wrong and harmful to that community without endeavoring to prevent it." [The Letters of John Wesley, III (Oxford: Oxford University Press, 1980), p.191]

Chapter Three

Demonstrations of judgment upon the Ungodly

5 Now I desire to remind you, though you know all things once for all, that the Lord, after saving a people out of the land of Egypt, subsequently destroyed those who did not believe. 6 And angels who did not keep their own domain, but abandoned their proper abode, He has kept in eternal bonds under darkness for the judgment of the great day, 7 just as Sodom and Gomorrah and the cities around them, since they in the same way as these indulged in gross immorality and went after strange flesh, are exhibited as an example in undergoing the punishment of eternal fire. 8 Yet in the same way these men, also by dreaming, defile the flesh, and reject authority, and revile angelic majesties.
Jude 1:5-8

A recent article in Reader's Digest poked fun at some labels that manufactures put on their products that state the obvious. Here's some of the labels they cited:

- On a portable stroller: "Caution: Remove infant before folding for storage."

- On a package of fireplace longs: "Caution risk of fire."
- On a hair dryer: "Do not use while sleeping.
  —Reader's Digest, April 2002, p. 60

At the risk of stating the obvious today, false teacher's will one day experience God's judgment.

AS SEEN IN THE EXODUS FROM SLAVERY

The Déjà vu [Day-ja-voo] (the experience of thinking that a new situation had occurred before).

Now I desire to remind you, though you know all things once for all - this promise of judgment wasn't anything new. We need to be reminded of things that we already know that is a ministry of the Holy Spirit. While the following verse has the Disciples in mind, it has application in a general sense to all believers.

"But the Helper, the Holy Spirit, whom the Father will send in My name, He will teach you all things, and bring to your remembrance all that I said to you." John 14:26

"Therefore, I will always be ready to remind you of these things, even though you already know them, and have been established in the truth which is present with you." 2 Peter 1:12

As the Vietnam Veteran's Memorial, that long wall of black marble engraved with the names of those killed in the war, we need to remember those destroyed by apostasy, also.

The *Deliverance*

that the Lord, after saving a people out of the land of Egypt - The idea here is that of deliverance from Egypt. The word "saved" has to be determined by its context. Not every place it's used, does it speak of being born-again or regenerated. It we make these people who were saved out of the land of Egypt, regenerated then they would be saved then lost (destroyed). That would contradict other scriptures. The context of Jude makes it clear that the destroyed are referring to false teachers, who were lost and thus headed for judgment. The Correlation with the other two demonstrations that of fallen angels and Sodom makes it clear the destruction is eternal. The "saved" here are not regenerated but delivered physically from Egyptian bondage.

"Now I want to remind you, though you were fully informed once for all, that though the Lord [at one time] delivered a people out of the land of Egypt, He subsequently destroyed those [of them] who did not believe [who refused to adhere to, trust in, and rely upon Him]." Jude 1:5 (AMP)

The entire nation was delivered from Egypt, but that does not mean that each individual was personally saved through faith in the Lord. Israel was delivered out of Egypt by the Ten Plagues and the Passover. In the Passover a lamb was sacrificed for each family. Physical deliverance would be for all who were inside, on which the blood had been put on the outside door post. But Spiritual deliverance was only for those who exercised faith in that provision. Same was true on the Day of Atonement, an animal sacrifice was offered for the entire nation, but only those who exercised faith in that provision were actually saved. When Israel was delivered from Egypt a "mixed multitude" went with them, a picture of the false teachers among true believers.

"A mixed multitude also went up with them, along with flocks and herds, a very large number of livestock." Exodus 12:38

In the Passover and the Day of Atonement, not all who partook were actually saved. Notice in the Passover they were eating the lamb which is a picture of believing (Jn. 6). The Disciples that followed Jesus for a time gladly ate of the physical bread Jesus provided. But when he talked of eating His flesh, a reference to believing on Him, they permanently forsook following Him. They were lost, at least for a time, among the saved. Some of those that ate of the lamb physically in the Passover, and were inside when the blood was applied to the outward doorpost, were lost among the saved. The false teachers, Jude warns will be lost among the saved.

"It follows, therefore, that not every circumcised member of Israel was truly circumcised in heart (Deut 10:16; 30:6; Jer. 4:4). Jude constructed an analogy between the saving of Israel out of Egypt (a physical act) and God's saving act in Jesus Christ, but we ought not necessarily to conclude from this that the Israelites liberated from Egypt were truly circumcised in heart, that they truly belonged to the people of God. Indeed, those who sinned in the wilderness and were then judged demonstrated that they did not truly belong to the Lord at all, that they did not have circumcised hearts in the first place. We ought not, then, construct a strict correspondence between the deliverance of Israel out of Egypt and the spiritual salvation of believers." [New American Commentary]

Like Judas many people are among the Delivered who are not really delivered at all. They have only a mere outward confession.

"7 "You hypocrites, rightly did Isaiah prophesy of you: 8 'THIS PEOPLE HONORS ME WITH THEIR LIPS, BUT THEIR HEART IS FAR AWAY FROM ME. 9 'BUT IN VAIN DO THEY WORSHIP ME, TEACHING AS DOCTRINES THE PRECEPTS OF MEN.'" Matthew 15:7-9

"They profess to know God, but by their deeds they deny Him, being detestable and disobedient and worthless for any good deed." Titus 1:16

Not everybody is who they appear to be! In the mid-1930's, British authorities had a surprise when the Canadian Pacific Liner, The Duchess of York, docked at Liverpool. Looking for American gangster John Dillinger, Scotland

Yard detectives made a thorough search of the ship. But they didn't find Dillinger. Instead, they found a Buddhist ecclesiastic, the abbot Jochao Chao-kung. But the British immediately recognized the oriental holy man as their old friend Ignatius Trebitsch Lincoln, one of the fantastic figures of the First World War, former British member of Parliament and also a German spy. He was most interesting, however, not in connection with espionage, but with religion. He was born a Jew, became a Lutheran missionary, then a Presbyterian, and later joined the Church of England, in which he became a curate. Then he turned Quaker. Next, he tried religion in the Orient. He also did some gunrunning and became financial adviser to a Chinese general. He had been prominent as a member of the imperial court of Manchukuo. And then he became a Buddhist monk. But Lincoln didn't stop there. In the last years of his life he was a double agent, spying both for and against Japan. The Japanese executed him in 1943 when they learned of his actions. False teachers can be masters of disguises...

The *Destruction*

subsequently destroyed - the entire congregation except for Joshua and Caleb were destroyed (Num. 14:35). Some were true believers and some were not. The true believers were physically destroyed but not spiritually and eternally; while the unbelievers were destroyed eternally. Jude by Context and Correlation of the two other examples is focusing on unbelievers. Point: Jude is telling them to watch for deception, just as false teachers crept in unnoticed among Israel, so they will in the Church. But their end will be judgment.

"...The false believers who had infiltrated God's people would be judged, just like the false believers who rejected God in the wilderness (see Num. 25:1-9)." [The Nelson Study Bible]

These false teachers want to infiltrate the church and take over! Imagine allowing an unsafe driver to drive a school bus - it would put everybody in jeopardy. According to V. Dion Haynes and Jim Mateja in the Chicago Tribune, some astonishing news came forth in the aftermath of the tragic auto accident that killed Princess Diana in 1997. The chauffeur of the car had three times the legal limit of alcohol in his bloodstream. Furthermore, police estimated the car had been going as fast as 120 miles per hour when the crash occurred in the Paris tunnel. Clearly the wrong man was at the wheel of the princess's car. But that is not unusual for celebrities, reported one security expert. Jerry Hoffman, president of a Cincinnati-based company that builds armored cars and trains drivers, said, "My experience is that a person will spend $150,000 to $200,000 on a limo and then spend no money on training the person to drive it. The driver is hired based on how friendly he is." How crazy to turn the church over to one who is spiritually reckless and has no personal relationship with Christ.

The result is that lost people will be deceived and eventually destroyed. Tony Evans notes, "WHAT happens to people who die without Christ? They go to hell! There is no respectable way to say it. They go to HELL. For how long? Forever! There is always the person who will say, "Wait a minute. I am not sure I believe in hell." This is one chance that may not be worth taking. Certain things you can afford to make a mistake on, but this isn't one of them. If a man doesn't have food, that's bad but he can recover from that. If a man doesn't live in a good house, that's bad but he can recover from that. If a man doesn't have the best clothes, that's bad but he can recover from that. If he doesn't have the job he prefers to have, that's bad but he can recover from that. If a man has to walk because he can't afford a car, that's bad but he can recover from that. No matter how bad a person's finances are, they can recover from that. But if a man dies without a personal relationship with Jesus Christ and wakes up in hell, that's a blow that he can never recover from."

The *Disbelief*

those who did not believe - "He who believes in the Son has everlasting life; and he who does not believe the Son shall not see life, but the wrath of God abides on him." (John 3:36). That is the only sin that condemns a person. The sad thing is that Jesus died on the cross for those false teachers also.

"But false prophets also arose among the people, just as there will also be false teachers among you, who will secretly introduce destructive heresies, even denying the Master *who bought them*, bringing swift destruction upon themselves." 2 Peter 2:1

"The price for the sins of all men (including these false teachers) was paid by the death of Christ, though no man can have benefit of this forgiveness except through faith in the Savior (see 1 Cor. 6:20; 1 Peter 1:18-19)." [Ryrie Study Bible]

This demonstration of judgment is one proof that the false teacher will ultimately face judgment. In fact all who reject Jesus Christ will face God's wrath. Today it looks like there is no sense of judgment, reminds of O. J. Simpson, he was found "not guilty" in the murder case of Nicole Brown Simpson and Ron Goldman. But judgment always comes sooner or later - First, another jury held him "liable" for the same crime. How could that be? There were different standards of proof. In the first trial, the standard was "beyond a reasonable doubt," while in the second trial it was "more likely than not." Then, in September 2007, Simpson was arrested in Las Vegas, Nevada, and charged with numerous felonies, including armed robbery and kidnapping. In 2008 he was found guilty and sentenced to 33 years imprisonment, with a minimum of 9 years without parole. He is currently serving his sentence at the Lovelock Correctional Center in Lovelock, Nevada. Finally, he still faces God's judgment, at the Great White Throne Judgment, if he dies without receiving Jesus Christ as his Savior.

AS SEEN IN THE EXPLUSION OF EVIL SPIRITS

Patricia Greenlee's son is a state trooper in West Virginia who recently gave a woman a ticket for going 15 miles over the speed limit. After handing her the ticket, she asked, "Don't you give out warnings?" "Yes ma'am," was his reply, "They're all up and down the road. They say, 'Speed Limit 55.'" Jude gives us warning all up and down this book about false teachers and their inevitable judgment. So we come to the Demonstrations of judgment on the Ungodly - The Expulsion of evil spirits. We have looked at the demonstration in the Exodus out of Egyptian Slavery; now the expulsion of evil spirits. Jude 6

THE ANGELS ORIGINAL STATURE

And angels who did not keep their own domain - two things to notice.

The *Doctrine* of Angels:

I. The Presence of Angels.
A. The Teaching of Scripture.
Existence taught in at least thirty-four books of Bible. The word
angel occurs about 275 times.
B. The Teaching of Savior.
Christ knew of and taught the existence of angels (Matthew 18:10; Matthew 26:53).
II. The Profile of Angels.
A. The Creation of Angels.
1. The Agent who created them – God

(Neh.9:6/Psa.148:2-5/Col. 1:16/etc.)

2. The Act of their creation - before the physical universe (Job 38:4-7).

3. The Assumptions: Created Instantaneously and simultaneously - they are a host not a race that perpetuates itself.

B. The Characteristics of angels.

1. Called Innumerable (Psa.68:17/Heb. 12:22/Jude 14/Rev.5:11)

The idea is that there are so many of them that man cannot count them, of course God knows the exact number.

2. They are Indestructible - they cannot die (Lu.20:34-36)

John Martin, "Jesus did not say that resurrected people become angels. His point was that they, like angels, will be immortal." Sumrall, "As one man put it, "angels never get sick, never go to the hospital, never die. You'll never read an obituary for an angel. You'll never go to an angel's funeral. God created angels to live forever."

3. Angels are Incapable of reproduction (Mt. 22:30). Since angels never die, there is no need for them to reproduce. Again, the resurrected believer in heaven will not marry either.

4. Angels were all Initially created good and holy.

God obviously could not create anything sinful!

5. Angels have Incredible power (Psa.

103:20/2 Pet.2:11).

6. Angels are Inferior to God.

a. They are limited by Space - only God is omnipresent.(Dan.9: 21-23)

b. They are limited in Strength - only God is omnipotent.

c. They are limited in Sense [understanding] - only God is omniscient.

7. Angels are Individuals. - Persons.

a. They have intellectual capacity (Eph. 3:10).

b. They have emotions (Lu. 2:9-14; 15:10).

c. They have a will (Jude 6).

8. The are Invisible - spirit beings (Heb. 1:14). They can take on some kind of visible form, often appearing as if they were a man. Gen.18:1-2, 16, 22

C. The Classification of angels:

- One Archangel Is Named, Michael (Jude 9).
- Chief Princes (Daniel 10:13).
- Ruling Angels (Ephes. 3:10).
- Guardian Angels (for all, Hebrews 1:14; for children, Matthew 18:10).
- Seraphim (Isaiah 6:1-3). Have to do with worship of God.
- Cherubim (Genesis 3:22-24). Guarding the holiness of God.
- Elect Angels (1 Tim. 5:21).

III. Thirdly, the Program of Angels.
A. To Savior.
1. Predicted His birth (Luke 1:26-33).
2. Proclaimed His birth (Luke 2:13).
3. Protected the Baby (Matthew 2:13).
4. Provided strength after temptation (Matthew 4:11).
5. Prepared to defend Him (Matthew 26:53).
6. Provided strength in Gethsemane (Luke 22:43).
7. Performed the act of rolling away stone from tomb (Matthew 28:2).
8. Proclaimed the Resurrection (Matthew 28:6).
9. Predicted His Return. (Ac.1:11).
10. Praise Him at His Return. (Heb.1:6)
B. To Saints.
1. The can Communicate with us (Ac.8:26; 10:1-8; 11:13-14; 27:22-25). Caution: Gal.1:8
2. They can Console us (Hebrews 1:14).
3. They can Care for us (Acts 5 &12/Mt.18:10).
4. They Consider us - interested in a. our Conduct (1 Cor.11:10; 4:9/1 Tim. 5:21); and b. Converts (Lu.12:8-9; 15:10).
5. Care for righteous at death (Luke 16:22; Jude 9).
C. To lost Sinners.
1. Announce impending judgments (Genesis 19:13; Rev. 14:6-7).

2. Accomplish punishment (Acts 12:23).
3. Act as reapers in the separation at end of the age (Matthew 13:39).
IV. Two basic Problems:
A. To Ignore them. We should acknowledge, appreciate, and admire their ministry.
B. To Idolize them. They are never to be worshiped! Col.2:18/Rev.19:10; 22:9

That is just a brief look at the Doctrine of angels.

The *Domain* of the angels

domain - 'Beginning, origin, authority, rule, domain, sphere of influence."

their proper abode - The word for "abode" or "habitation." It means a dwelling place. It refers here to the heavenly region, the abode that God planned and prepared for those angelic beings. The only other time the word occurs is in connection with "our house which is from heaven" (2 Cor. 5:2), a reference to the spiritual, heavenly bodies that we shall inhabit one day. They were once pure, holy, and living in God's presence, in positions of authority, enjoying God...

DEPARTURE OF SOME ANGELS

but abandoned their proper abode - Some
Bible students believe that Jude was teaching
not only a revolt of the angels against God,
but also an invasion of earth by these fallen
angels. They point to Genesis 6:1-4 and claim
that "the sons of God" were fallen angels who
assumed human bodies, cohabited with the
daughters of men, and produced a race of
giants on the earth. This was one reason that
God sent the Flood. There are several
problems with this view:

- While it is true that "the sons of God"
  is a title for angels (Job 1:6; 2:1;
  38:7), it is a title used only for unfallen
  angels.
- The judgment from the rebellion of
  Gen.6 fell solely on human beings, no
  mention of angels at all.
- As we have seen angels are spirits and
  do not have bodies. In the Old
  Testament record, we do read of
  angels who appeared in human form,
  but this was not incarnation. How
  could a spirit being have a physical
  relationship with a woman, even if that
  being assumed a temporary body of
  some kind? Our Lord taught that the

angels do not engage in sex. (Matt. 22:30).

- Some try to take the "just as" and "in same way" and say that just as the men of Sodom went after strange flesh [homosexuality] so these fallen angels went after strange flesh - human being; But it can be simply saying that both angels and those of Sodom are examples of God's judgment.
- Genesis 6:4 presents a strong argument against the view that fallen angels cohabited with women and produced a race of giants. "There were giants in the earth in those days; and also after that'. This would mean that a second invasion of fallen angels had to take place! We have no record of this in Scripture.
- I do not think anybody reading Gen.6 would normally identify the "sons of God" with fallen angels. You have to use isogesis - reading something into the text.

Many good Bible teachers tie this into Gen. 6, but I personally feel like McShane who writes:

"It is not easy for some of us to believe that sexless spirits would lust after women and that they would vacate heaven in order to gratify their passion. It takes some stretch of imagination to conceive that bodiless beings could be plagued with fleshly lusts. Is it not strange that it took almost 1000 years for them to behold the beauty of women? Why did they not take hold of Eve, for they witnessed her creation, and she must have been the most beautiful of all women? Are we to think that their heavenly abode meant so little to them as to leave it to become subjects of the limitations of a cursed earth?"

This takes us back to Lucifer's rebellion and fall. (Isaiah 14:12-17; Ezekiel 28:12-19) At the time of Lucifer's fall he persuaded one third (Revelation 12:4) of the angels of heaven to rebel with him.

3Then another sign appeared in heaven: and behold, a great red dragon having seven heads and ten horns, and on his heads were seven diadems. 4 And his tail swept away a third of the stars of heaven and threw them to the earth. And the dragon stood before the woman who was about to give birth, so that when she gave birth he might devour her child." Revelation 12:3-4

These fallen angels are of course demons.

"Then He will also say to those on His left,

'Depart from Me, accursed ones, into the eternal fire which has been prepared for the devil and his angels;" Matthew 25:41

These fallen angels no longer have their stature with God in a heavenly position.

THEIR *CAPTURE*

He has kept in eternal bonds under darkness – Phillips notes, "Moreover, they are kept "under darkness." The word for "darkness" is zophos, which refers to the gloom of the underworld, to "nether darkness, murkiness, thick gloom." Both Jude and Peter use the word (Jude 6, 13; 2 Peter 2:14, 17). The word also is found in Hebrews 12:18, where it describes the awesome darkness that wrapped Sinai in its terrible embrace when God gave Moses the Law. How terrible must be the torment of these fallen beings! Once they dwelled in a light beyond the brightness of the noonday sun. Once they sang the praises of God in a land of bliss. Once they knew "joy unspeakable and full of glory." Once they gazed upon the throne of God and shouted for joy at the wonders of His works in creation...But now all they know is [darkness]...and the terrible anticipation of "the judgment of the great day." The horror of that judgment is already upon them. If the terror of their coming doom haunts the demons (Matt. 8:28-29), how much more it must haunt these former sons of light, chained already in darkness and doomed to endure "the blackness of darkness forever."

- Apparently some of the angels that fell are now permanently confined (2 Pet. 2:4). That is what Jude 6 indicates. Some take it more as a future tense, Kistemaker, "We should not interpret this text to mean that all fallen angels are locked up in a certain place. If this were the case, the earth would not be plagued by demons. This picture Jude conveys is that the rebellious angels are living in spiritual darkness and are chained to their sentence of divine judgment from which they can never escape." Personally I believe that some of the angels are now permanently confined, but not all of them. Why some are and others are not? I do not know - maybe like some people are confined in jail and some are not? Lu.8:31

- Others are now temporarily confined. Rev. 9:1-15

- Many are freely moving about! Eph. 6:11-12

Those in our passage have been captured and are now being kept in eternal bonds.

THEIR *FUTURE*

for the judgment of the great day - there is a future day of judgment in which all fallen angels, including these, will end up in the Lake of Fire - Hell. Judgment of Fallen Angels:

1. Time? Probably after the Millennium.
2. Place. Unspecified.
3. Judges. Christ and believers (1 Cor. 6:3).
4. Subjects judged. Fallen angels.
5. Basis. Disobedience to God in following Satan in his revolt.
6. Result. Cast into the lake of fire.
7. Scripture. Jude 6; 1 Cor. 6:3.

The point - it is a warning to the false teachers that they cannot avoid the judgment of God.

"4 For if God did not spare angels when they sinned, but cast them into hell and committed them to chains of gloomy darkness to be kept until the judgment; 5 if he did not spare the ancient world, but preserved Noah, a herald of righteousness, with seven others, when he brought a flood upon the world of the ungodly; 6 if by turning the cities of Sodom and Gomorrah to ashes he condemned them to extinction, making them an example of what is going to happen to the ungodly;" 2 Peter 2:4-6 (ESV)

The warning if even the mighty angels could not escape the judgment of God, what makes the false teachers think they can! Their judgment will not occur without sufficient warnings. A 22-year-old man climbed an electrical tower in Clarksville, Indiana and survived a 69,000-volt shock that a utility official said was nearly always fatal. Jason Grisham "appeared to have extensive burn marks on his chest and his pants appeared to have exploded," police said. Grisham, from neighboring New Albany, scaled the fence around the tower about 6:30 a.m. and then started to climb the tower itself, rising 12 to 15 feet before he "received a dose of... electricity and was knocked to the ground," The incident disrupted power to 6,800 customers. The fence Grisham climbed was 7 feet tall and has three strands of barbed wire on top of it, and there are clearly visible signs saying "Danger/High Voltage," Who cannot blame Jason for getting zapped? Same with these false teachers, they have nobody to blame but themselves.

AS IN THE EXECUTION OF SODOM AND GOMORRAH

Demonstrations of judgment to the ungodly is seen in the Execution of Sodom and Gomorrah. We have seen judgment in the Exodus out of Egyptian Slavery; in the Explusion of the evil Spirits; and now in the Execution of Sodom (Jude 6).

THE CITIES ON THE *PLAIN*

just as Sodom and Gomorrah and the cities around them, since they in the same way as these - Just as - As with the unfaithful Israelites and the rebellious angels (vv. 5-6), so also the people of Sodom and Gomorrah (Genesis 19) received the judgment of eternal fire [ESV Study Bible]. No other incident in history is used more than Sodom and Gomorrah as an example of God's judgment:

"22 "Now the generation to come, your sons who rise up after you and the foreigner who comes from a distant land, when they see the plagues of the land and the diseases with which the LORD has afflicted it, will say, 23 'All its land is brimstone and salt, a burning waste, unsown and unproductive, and no grass grows in it, like the overthrow of Sodom and

Gomorrah, Admah and Zeboiim, which the LORD overthrew in His anger and in His wrath.'" Deuteronomy 29:22-23

31 "Indeed their rock is not like our Rock, Even our enemies themselves judge this. 32 "For their vine is from the vine of Sodom, And from the fields of Gomorrah; Their grapes are grapes of poison, Their clusters, bitter. Deuteronomy 32:31-32

"Unless the LORD of hosts Had left us a few survivors, We would be like Sodom, We would be like Gomorrah." Isaiah 1:9

"The expression of their faces bears witness against them, And they display their sin like Sodom; They do not even conceal it. Woe to them! For they have brought evil on themselves." Isaiah 3:9

"And Babylon, the beauty of kingdoms, the glory of the Chaldeans' pride, Will be as when God overthrew Sodom and Gomorrah." Isaiah 13:19

"Also among the prophets of Jerusalem I have seen a horrible thing: The committing of adultery and walking in falsehood; And they strengthen the hands of evildoers, So that no one has turned back from his wickedness. All of them have become to Me like Sodom, And her inhabitants like Gomorrah." Jeremiah 23:14

"17 "Edom will become an object of horror; everyone who passes by it will be horrified and will hiss at all its wounds. 18 "Like the overthrow of Sodom and Gomorrah with its neighbors," says the LORD, "no one will live there, nor will a son of man reside in it." Jeremiah 49:17-18

"For the iniquity of the daughter of my people Is greater than the sin of Sodom, Which was overthrown as in a moment, And no hands were turned toward her." Lamentations 4:6

"I overthrew you, as God overthrew Sodom and Gomorrah, And you were like a firebrand snatched from a blaze; Yet you have not returned to Me," declares the LORD." Amos 4:11

"Therefore, as I live," declares the LORD of hosts, The God of Israel, "Surely Moab will be like Sodom And the sons of Ammon like Gomorrah— A place possessed by nettles and salt pits, And a perpetual desolation. The remnant of My people will plunder them And the remainder of My nation will inherit them." Zephaniah 2:9

"Truly I say to you, it will be more tolerable for the land of Sodom and Gomorrah in the day of judgment than for that city." Matthew 10:15

23 "And you, Capernaum, will not be exalted to heaven, will you? You will descend to Hades; for if the miracles had occurred in Sodom which occurred in you, it would have remained to this day. 24 "Nevertheless I say to you that it will be more tolerable for the land of Sodom in the day of judgment, than for you." Matthew 11:23-24

"10 "But whatever city you enter and they do not receive you, go out into its streets and say, 11 'Even the dust of your city which clings to our feet we wipe off in protest against you; yet be sure of this, that the kingdom of God has come near.' 12 "I say to you, it will be more tolerable in that day for Sodom than for that city." Luke 10:10-12

"22 And He said to the disciples, "The days will come when you will long to see one of the days of the Son of Man, and you will not see it. 23 "They will say to you, 'Look there! Look here!' Do not go away, and do not run after them. 24 "For just like the lightning, when it flashes out of one part of the sky, shines to the other part of the sky, so will the

Son of Man be in His day. 25 "But first He must suffer many things and be rejected by this generation. 26 "And just as it happened in the days of Noah, so it will be also in the days of the Son of Man: 27 they were eating, they were drinking, they were marrying, they were being given in marriage, until the day that Noah entered the ark, and the flood came and destroyed them all. 28 "It was the same as happened in the days of Lot: they were eating, they were drinking, they were buying, they were selling, they were planting, they were building; 29 but on the day that Lot went out from Sodom it rained fire and brimstone from heaven and destroyed them all." Luke 17:22-29

"And just as Isaiah foretold, "UNLESS THE LORD OF SABBATH HAD LEFT TO US A POSTERITY, WE WOULD HAVE BECOME LIKE SODOM, AND WOULD HAVE RESEMBLED GOMORRAH." Romans 9:29

"and if He condemned the cities of Sodom and Gomorrah to destruction by reducing them to ashes, having made them an example to those who would live ungodly lives thereafter;" 2 Peter 2:6

THE CITIES OF *PERVERSION*

Unrestrained

indulged in gross immorality - It means to "Indulge in sexual immorality, give oneself to fornication." This is an intensified form of the verb porneuō (4062), "to commit fornication," and points to excessive indulgence in and giving oneself completely to immorality. It is used only once in the New Testament.

Years ago I heard Paul Harvey give an illustration of being consumed by lust:

First, the Eskimo coats his knife blade with animal blood and allows it to freeze. Then he adds another layer of blood, and another, until the blade is completely concealed by frozen blood. Next, the hunter fixes his knife in the ground with the blade up. When a wolf follows his sensitive nose to the source of the scent and discovers the bait, he licks it, tasting the fresh frozen blood. He begins to lick faster, more and more vigorously, lapping the blade until the keen edge is bare. Feverishly now, harder and harder the wolf licks the blade in the arctic night. So great becomes his craving for blood that the wolf does not notice the razor-sharp sting of the naked blade on his own tongue, nor does he recognize the instant at which his insatiable thirst is being satisfied by his OWN warm blood. His carnivorous appetite just craves more—until the dawn finds him dead in the snow!

"But put on the Lord Jesus Christ, and make no provision for the flesh in regard to its lusts." Romans 13:14

"Now flee from youthful lusts and pursue righteousness, faith, love and peace, with those who call on the Lord from a pure heart." 2 Timothy 2:22

"15 Do not love the world nor the things in the world. If anyone loves the world, the love of the Father is not in him. 16 For all that is in the world, the lust of the flesh and the lust of the eyes and the boastful pride of life, is not from the Father, but is from the world. 17 The world is passing away, and also its lusts; but the one who does the will of God lives forever." 1 John 2:15-17

Unnatural

and went after strange flesh - strange is "other." ἕτερος heteros adj. This word must be studied in conjunction with its synonym, allos

(241). Although sometimes a distinction is hard to see, where they are used together, allos means: (1) "one" of a series; and (2) "another" of a similar nature. On the other hand, heteros is used to indicate: (1) "one" of two, and thus (2) "another" of a dissimilar nature. Thus Luke 23:32 says "two other (heteroi) men, both criminals," were also led out to be crucified with Jesus. In Matthew 11:3 Jesus was asked if He is the One that should come, or do we look for another (different) One. In Mark 16:12 Jesus is said to have appeared in another (different) form (i.e., in one He had not assumed before) in His resurrection appearance. Heteros can also mean neighbor or one other than oneself (e.g., 1 Corinthians 6:1; 10:24,29; 14:17; Galatians 6:4). The "otherness" expressed by heteros explains a great deal in the New Testament. To "speak in other tongues" (lalein heterais glōssais) thus means to speak in a language different from one's own (Acts 2:4). And "others" (heteroi; i.e., those who were unbelievers) said that those who received the Spirit at Pentecost were drunk with new wine, denying the work of the Spirit. In the same manner Paul inquired of the Galatians as to why they departed from the grace of God to another, that is, different (heteros) gospel

(Galatians 1:6); which is not another (allos, "similar") (Galatians 1:7)." [Complete Biblical Library]

Kistemaker, "What is Jude saying?...In the context of the verse, the position of the pronoun these indicates that Jude refers to the men of Sodom. But what is the meaning of the term other flesh? The Greek reveals that in the case of duality [for example, male and female] the word other can mean "a second of two" and in the context denotes a difference of kind. [Robertson, Grammar, p.748].Therefore, when the men of Sodom were interested in sexual relationships with men, they perverted the created order of natural intercourse. That is, the men of Sodom did not desire females (see. Gen. 19:8-9); instead, these men demanded homosexual relations with the men who visited Lot. The activity of the Sodomites is perversion."

So the strange flesh is another of a different kind - based on the account of Gen. 19:5 this is referring to homosexual behavior. A man having sex with another man is a man going after a different flesh then normal - a man normally goes after a woman.

"[The wicked are sentenced to suffer] just as Sodom and Gomorrah and the adjacent towns—which likewise gave themselves over to impurity and indulged in unnatural vice and sensual perversity..." Jude 1:7 (AMP)

"just as Sodom and Gomorrah and the surrounding cities, which likewise indulged in sexual immorality and pursued unnatural desire..." Jude 1:7 (ESV)

"And don't forget the cities of Sodom and Gomorrah and their neighboring towns, all full of lust of every kind, including lust of men for other men..." Jude 1:7 (TLB)

McShane, "The inhabitants of these cities threw off all restraint and let their passions drive them into the basest of sins, so that to this day sodomy is used as equivalent to homosexuality. The climax of these evil men mentioned in verse 4 ["certain persons crept in unnoticed"] is here reached...so the "sexual immorality and going after strange flesh" describes both the men of Sod and the evil workers Jude wrote about. This is the first of seven references to "these" - vv. 8, 10, 12, 14, 16 and 19. Some have tried to distinguish this first one from the others and make it refer to the angels, but this is inconsistent with the normal style of the epistle and leads to all kinds of strange ideas."

The Bible is clear about homosexuality:

"22 'You shall not lie with a male as one lies with a female; it is an abomination. Leviticus 18:22-23

"26 For this reason God gave them over to degrading passions; for their women exchanged the natural function for that which is unnatural, 27 and in the same way also the men abandoned the natural function of the woman and burned in their desire toward one another, men with men committing indecent acts and receiving in their own persons the due penalty of their error." Romans 1:26-27

"9 Or do you not know that the unrighteous will not inherit the kingdom of God? Do not be deceived; neither fornicators, nor idolaters, nor adulterers, nor effeminate, nor homosexuals, 10 nor thieves, nor the covetous, nor drunkards, nor revilers, nor swindlers, will inherit the kingdom of God." 1 Corinthians 6:9-10

"9 realizing the fact that law is not made for a righteous person, but for those who are lawless and rebellious, for the ungodly and sinners, for the unholy and profane, for those who kill their fathers or mothers, for murderers 10 and immoral men and homosexuals and kidnappers and liars and perjurers, and whatever else is contrary to sound teaching," 1 Timothy 1:9-10

Both our Military and the sanction of Marriage are being threatened by the invasion of this vile perversion.

CITIES UNDER DIVINE *PUNISHMENT*

are exhibited as an example in undergoing the punishment of eternal fire – God's judgment is eternal!

Wiersbe, "These are examples, "Both Peter and Jude state that God made these cities an example to warn the ungodly that God does indeed judge sin (see 2 Peter 2:6). When you combine their descriptions, you discover that the citizens of Sodom and Gomorrah (and the other cities involved) were: ungodly, filthy, wicked, unlawful, unjust, and given over to fornication. They did not occasionally commit unnatural sexual sins; they indulged in them and gave themselves over to the pursuit of lust. The Greek verb is intensive: "to indulge in excessive immorality." This was their way of life—and death! Strange flesh means "different flesh." The bent of their life was constantly downward, indulging in unnatural acts (see Rom. 1:24-27). Those who hold the "fallen angel" interpretation of Genesis 6 make the "strange flesh" refer to angels in human form; but when did the angels invade Sodom and Gomorrah? And, if fallen angels are meant, how can their sin and the sin of the Sodomites apply to us today, for we have no fallen angels to tempt or seduce us? Indeed, the men at Lot's door did want to engage in homosexual activity with his angelic guests, but the Sodomites did not know they were angels. Another possibility is that the Sodomites were guilty not only of unnatural sex with each other, but also with animals, which would be "strange flesh." Both homosexuality and bestiality are condemned by God (Lev. 18:22-25).These cities were set forth by God as an example and warning to ungodly people today. The verb set forth means "to expose openly to public view." (Interestingly enough, the word was used to describe a corpse lying in state!) But the cities of the plain are not today in public view. It is generally agreed among archeologists that Sodom and Gomorrah are buried under the southern end of the Dead

Sea. How, then, do they serve as an example? In the pages of the Word of God. No one can read Genesis 18-19 without clearly seeing God's hatred for sin and, at the same time, His patience and willingness to postpone judgment. This certainly ties in with Peter's explanation for God's seeming delay in fulfilling the promise of Christ's return (2 Peter 3:8ff). The sin of Israel was rebellious unbelief (Heb. 3:12). The sin of the angels was rebellion against the throne of God. The sin of Sodom and Gomorrah was indulging in unnatural lust. Unbelief, rebellion against authority, and sensual indulgence were sins characteristic of the false teachers. The conclusion is obvious: the apostates will be judged. But, meanwhile, God's soldiers must stay on duty and see to it that these false teachers do not creep into the ranks and start to lead people astray. "Take heed unto thyself, and unto the doctrine" (1 Tim. 4:16). [Bible Exposition Commentary]

The specified duration of hell:

- Everlasting punishment (Mt. 25:46).
- Eternal judgment (Heb. 6:1-2).
- Everlasting destruction (2 Thess. 1:0).
- Eternal fire:("Gehenna") (Mt. 18:8-9; 25:41).
- Unquenchable fire (Mk. 9:42-48).

- Eternal torment (Revelation 19:20; 20:10).

The poisons these false teachers are dishing out will one day be served to them! They may appear to be getting away with murder now - but one day all of that will end. Oklahoma City, OK (AP)—Nannie Doss, described as "a self-made widow who fed rat poison to four of her five husbands, 60-year-old, jovial, gum-chewing widow died at University Hospital which she entered May 20 after becoming ill at the state penitentiary at McAlester. She was sentenced to life imprisonment for the murder of her fifth husband, Samuel L. Doss. But in addition to him, she also admitted feeding lethal doses of poison to three more husbands.

HUSBAND NO. 1, Charles Braggs, was the lone survivor. He married Nannie in Blue Mountain, Alabama, and divorced her when he said he thought the food he was eating didn't "taste right."

HUSBAND NO. 2, Frank Harrelson, Jacksonville, Alabama, was poisoned simply because Nannie said she heard he made arrangements to leave her and he also "ran around." She used rat poison in his corn liquor.

HUSBAND NO. 3, Harley Lanning, was obtained in Lexington, North Carolina, and died afterward. Nannie said she married him while still in "deep mourning" for Harrelson. Later she wanted to be through with romance because "the Lord had taken two of my husbands away."

HUSBAND NO. 4, Richard Louis Morton, Emporia, Kansas, was the result of a mail-order courtship. He died suddenly, a few months after he refused to let her visit relatives in North Carolina.

HUSBAND NO. 5, Doss, was dying at Tulsa when Nannie was corresponding with prospective Husband No. 6, James H. Keel, Goldsboro, North Carolina, through a lonely-hearts' club.

Chapter Four

Depiction of false teachers

8 *Yet in the same way these men, also by dreaming, defile the flesh, and reject authority, and revile angelic majesties.* 9 *But Michael the archangel, when he disputed with the devil and argued about the body of Moses, did not dare pronounce against him a railing judgment, but said, "The Lord rebuke you!"* 10 *But these men revile the things which they do not understand; and the things which they know by instinct, like unreasoning animals, by these things they are destroyed.* 11 *Woe to them! For they have gone the way of Cain, and for pay they have rushed headlong into the error of Balaam, and perished in the rebellion of Korah.* 12 *These are the men who are hidden reefs in your love feasts when they feast with you without fear, caring for themselves; clouds without water, carried along by winds; autumn trees without fruit, doubly dead, uprooted;* 13 *wild waves of the sea, casting up their own shame like foam; wandering stars, for whom the black darkness has been reserved forever.* 14 *It was also about these men that Enoch, in the seventh*

generation from Adam, prophesied, saying, "Behold, the Lord came with many thousands of His holy ones, ^{15} to execute judgment upon all, and to convict all the ungodly of all their ungodly deeds which they have done in an ungodly way, and of all the harsh things which ungodly sinners have spoken against Him." ^{16} These are grumblers, finding fault, following after their own lusts; they speak arrogantly, flattering people for the sake of gaining an advantage. Jude 1:8-16

Oscar Wilde's book, The Picture of Dorian Gray, begins with an artist finishing a portrait of a handsome man named Dorian Gray. Dorian loves the picture but is grieved by the realization that the picture will depict him as young - but he himself is doomed to become old and ugly. He gives his soul in exchange for the portrait getting old, while he himself stays young. Dorian lives a life of self-indulgence. He notices that the portrait is changing, aging, becoming cruel looking. He remains young and handsome but becomes fearful that someone might see the portrait and know about his true self - so he hides it. Years go by, marked by unrestrained sin, the portrait grows more and more hideous and grotesque. He one day views the portrait and in rage takes a knife and slashes the picture to pieces. His servants find Dorian, they find the slashed portrait which now pictures a young handsome man;

while lying on the floor a dead Dorian - old and repulsive, no longer recognizable to them. This is the way of false teachers, they seek to hide their true appearance. They look inviting, successful, and godly on the surface, but Jude brings before us a true portrait of their lives.

THE DEPICTION OF THE FALSE TEACHERS
WORLD

Their world is based on *Unreliable* revelation

Yet in the same way these men, also by dreaming - "Yet in like manner these people also, relying on their dreams..." Jude 8 ESV

"25 "I have heard what the prophets have said who prophesy falsely in My name, saying, 'I had a dream, I had a dream!' 26 "How long? Is there anything in the hearts of the prophets who prophesy falsehood, even these prophets of the deception of their own heart, 27 who intend to make My people forget My name by their dreams which they relate to one another, just as their fathers forgot My name because of Baal? 28 "The prophet who has a dream may relate his dream, but let him who has My word speak My word in truth. What does straw have in common with grain?" declares the LORD." Jeremiah 23:25-28

"Sigmund Freud made dreams popular in this century, teaching that dreams may hold the key to some of life's problems if they could be correctly deciphered. Carl Jung felt that certain symbols in dreams had great significance for understanding mankind's collective consciousness. Dreams are certainly elusive—in fact, one popular song speaks about "my elusive dream." Indeed, dreams fascinate people and everyone has had a distinctive dream or two that they remember. Dreams fade away, fly away and are transient (Ps. 73:20). They can be brought on by anxiety and care and create fear (Job 4:13; 7:14). They can also be produced by our minds as a delusion (Jer. 23:25-27)—a charge Jeremiah hurled against false prophets...The author of Ecclesiastes stated succinctly that many dreams and a lot of talk are meaningless, "For in many dreams and in many words there is emptiness. Rather, fear God." (Ecclesiastes 5:7). Believers should study how God used dreams in the Bible, but also realize that trusting in prayer and the Word is a much more foolproof way of discerning God's will for our lives." [Cross-reference Explorer]

"False teachers often claim dreams as the authoritative, divine source for their "new truths," which are really just lies and distortions. Such claims allow apostates to substitute their own counterfeit authority for God's true scriptural authority. Dreaming surely also includes apostates' perverted, evil imaginations. Rejecting the Word of God, they base their deceptive teachings on the misguided musings of their own deluded and demonized minds." [MacArthur New Testament Commentary]

"Let no one keep defrauding you of your prize by delighting in self-abasement and the worship of the angels, taking his stand on visions he has seen, inflated without cause by his fleshly mind," Colossians 2:18

Wiersbe said, "These people live in a dream world of unreality and delusion." They have been deluded by Satan regarding their beliefs and rejection of Divine truth. They think their present practices are okay. They do not expect judgment for their evil ways." Once we allow someone to exercise authority based on some supposed dream instead of the world of God they become little dictators! Their word instead of God's becomes the final say so. In Cuba, nothing is bigger than baseball, not even the cigars. Nothing, that is, except Castro. Once, he grabbed an aluminum bat and walked to the plate in an exhibition game against Venezuela. When Castro approached the batter's box, the president of Venezuela, Hugo Chavez, left his first-base position to take the mound. His first pitch didn't even reach the plate, and Castro kept his bat on his shoulder. The next pitch Castro swung and missed. A couple more balls and an attempted bunt later, the two heads of state were locked into a full count. Castro watched the 3-2 pitch sail through the middle of the strike zone and listened as the umpire called him out. "No," Castro said, "that was a ball." And he took first base. No one argued. President Chavez said nothing. The opposing team said nothing, and the umpire said nothing. Later Castro joked, "Today just wasn't his [President Chavez's] day." It is hard to argue with a false teacher, when we allow his/her words to overrule God's Word.

Their world is *Unclean*

These dreams seek to give them authority for their ungodly behavior, "The NIV translates the participle enypniazomenoi as "dreamers." This is fitting as long as the participle is understood to modify all three verbs, and the dreams are understood as the basis for the moral baseness of the opponents. They appealed to their dreams as a source of revelation, as a justification for their lifestyle." [New American Commentary] *defile the flesh* - bad beliefs always lead to bad behavior. "Flesh (sarx) refers here to the physical body. The word translated defile is from the verb miainō, which means to dye or stain something, such as clothing or glass. In addition, it can mean "to pollute," "to contaminate," "to soil," or "to corrupt." When linked with sarx, the reference is to moral and physical defilement, or sexual sin. Apostate teachers are inevitably immoral, because they are "devoid of the Spirit" (v. 19), thus they have no divine power to control their own sinful impulses (cf. Rom. 6:20-21; 8:7-8; Gal. 5:19)." McDonald, "Their thought life is polluted. Living in a world of filthy fantasies, they eventually find fulfillment of their dreams in sexual immorality." A filthy mind will produce a polluted body.

Cotton Patch, "And so it is with these fellows I'm warning you about. With their imaginations they debase the human body."

See, Rom. 12:1/1 Cor. 6:19-20/etc.

According to an October 29, 1994, story from the Reuters news agency, a Chinese woman named Zhang Meihua began to suffer mysterious symptoms when she turned twenty. She was losing the ability to nimbly move her legs and arms. Doctors could not find the cause, and the symptoms continued. Two decades passed, and Zhang began to also suffer from chronic headaches. Again she sought help from the doctors. This time a CAT scan and an X ray found the source of the woman's mysterious symptoms. A rusty pin was lodged in her head. The head of the pin was outside the skull, and the shaft penetrated into her brain. Doctors performed surgery and successfully extracted the pin. The doctors expressed amazement that the woman "could live for so long a time with a rusty pin stuck in her brain." After noting the position of the pin in her skull, they speculated that the pin had entered her skull sometime soon after birth and before her skull had hardened. Zhang, now fully recovered, said she "had no memory of being pierced by a pin in the head." Like the rusty pin in that woman's brain, these false teachers have impure thoughts lodged in their minds and it had an impact on their lives.

Their world is *Unruly*

and reject authority - The same Greek word is used here which occurs in 2 Peter 2:10, "and especially those who indulge the flesh in its corrupt desires and despise authority." The word, reject means "to have contempt; to scorn; to disdain; to have the lowest opinion of." The word occurs sixteen times in twelve passages. It can be translated "to count as nothing." Paul uses the word in the statement, "I will destroy the wisdom of the wise, and bring to nothing the understanding of the prudent" (1 Cor. 1:19; cf. Isa. 29:14). Here the word can be translated "to annul." The word for "dominion" [authority] refers to lordship, power, and dominion, whether angelic or human. It can be rendered "government." The brand of apostasy mentioned here disregards and seeks the overthrow of governments. Its followers disrespect government and promote sedition against lawful authority." "This is the apostate's attitude toward all God-ordained authority. As a result of living in their dream world, they arrogantly refuse to recognize God-ordained authority. God has clearly established a system of authority. (1) God Himself is the ultimate authority (Deuteronomy 11:27; Jeremiah 11:4, 7; Zechariah 6:15); (2)God has given authority to husbands (Ephesians 5:22-23, 1 Peter 3:1); (3) to parents (Ephesians 6:1, Colossians 3:20) and (4) to government (Romans 13:1-7) (5) He has also given authority to pastors (Hebrews 13:7, 17). Our God is a God of order and, to have order, there must be authority. You can tell a whole lot about a person by how he respects and responds to authority. Apostates despise authority." [Expository Pulpit Series]

Especially they had no regard for God's authority. Reminds me of four rabbis who had a series of debates, and 3 were always in accord against the fourth. One day, the rabbi, after the usual "3 to 1, majority rules" decided to appeal to a higher authority. He prayed, "Oh, God! I know in my heart that I am right and they are wrong! Please give me a sign to prove it to them!" It was a beautiful, sunny day. As soon as the rabbi finished his prayer, a storm cloud moved across the sky above the four. It rumbled once and dissolved. "A sign from God! See, I'm right, I knew it!"
But the other three disagreed, pointing out that storm clouds form on hot days. So the rabbi prayed again: "Oh, God, I need a bigger sign to show that I am right and they are wrong. So please, God, a bigger sign!" This time four storm clouds appeared, rushed toward each other to form one big cloud, and a bolt of lightning slammed into a tree on a nearby hill. "I told you I was right!" cried the rabbi, but his friends insisted that nothing had happened that could not be explained by natural causes. The rabbi was getting ready to ask for a very big sign, but just as he said, "Oh God...," the sky turned pitch black, the earth shook, and a deep, booming voice

intoned, "HE'S RIGHT!"

Then the spokesman for the 3 rabbi's put his hands on his hips, turned to the 1 lone rabbi and said, "So, now it's 3 to 2."

False prophets have little or no regard for God or his delegated authority. False teachers are depicted as Unreliable; Unclean; and Unruly. But you can only get that picture from God's Word. False teachers like Dorian Gray are not what they appear to be. Through its laws, our country declares it a crime to lie about the contents in a box of cereal. These laws demand that the outside of the package tell the truth about what is on the inside. Deceptive packaging is illegal. "Truth in advertising" regulations are another way to protect the public. A good example of this is the warning on a pack of cigarettes: "Smoking causes lung cancer, heart disease, emphysema, and may complicate pregnancy." Unfortunately, there are no such laws about people. We require no one to tell what really lies behind the packaging—the clothes, facial expressions, mannerisms, speech patterns, or affected behavior. No one is forced to tell you what he or she is really feeling, thinking, or planning to do. But the good news for us is that the word of God tells us the truth behind the lies on the outside of the false teacher, thus we have a divine label to show us what's really behind the smooth advertising.

FALSE TEACHERS *WORDS*

A false teacher is quick to flatter and exalt people for his own gain. But once he has exploited a person, the deceiver's flowery words quickly change to expose his true heart. Some time ago, the Saturday Evening Post ran a humorous article that traced the tendency for marriage partners to drift from a height of bliss into the humdrum of routine attitudes. Called "The Seven Ages of the Married Cold," the article likens the state of the marriage to the reaction of a husband to his wife's colds during seven years of marriage.

- The first year: "Sugar dumpling, I'm worried about my baby girl. You've got a bad sniffle and there's no telling about these things with all this strep around. I'm putting you in the hospital this afternoon for a general checkup and a good rest. I know the food's lousy, but I'll bring your meals from Rossini's. I've already got it arranged with the floor superintendent."

- The second year: "Listen darling, I don't like the sound of that cough and I've called Doc Miller to rush over here. Now you go to bed like a good girl, please? Just for Papa."

- The third year: "Maybe you'd better lie down, honey; nothing like having a little rest when you feel punk. I'll bring you something to eat. Have we got any soup?"
- The fourth year: "Look dear, be sensible. After you feed the kids and get the dishes washed, you'd better hit the sack."
- The fifth year: "Why don't you get yourself a couple of aspirin?"
- The sixth year: "If you'd just gargle or something, instead of sitting around barking like a seal!"
- The seventh year: "For Pete's sake, stop sneezing! Whatcha trying to do, gimme pneumonia?"

The false teacher's words sooner or later reveal their true heart. We are looking at a depiction of these false teachers; we looked at their World and now their Words.

THE *CONCEPT*

and speak evil - this verb is to Blaspheme, speak evil of, speak abusively, slander. It was a very serious sin when aimed at God:

"10 Now the son of an Israelite woman, whose father was an Egyptian, went out among the children of Israel; and this Israelite woman's son and a man of Israel fought each other in the camp. 11 And the Israelite woman's son blasphemed the name of the Lord and cursed; and so they brought him to Moses. (His mother's name was Shelomith the daughter of Dibri, of the tribe of Dan.) 12 Then they put him in custody, that the mind of the LORD might be shown to them. 13 And the LORD spoke to Moses, saying, 14 "Take outside the camp him who has cursed; then let all who heard him lay their hands on his head, and let all the congregation stone him. 15 Then you shall speak to the children of Israel, saying: 'Whoever curses his God shall bear his sin.

16 And whoever blasphemes the name of the LORD shall surely be put to death. All the congregation shall certainly stone him, the stranger as well as him who is born in the land. When he blasphemes the name of the Lord, he shall be put to death." Leviticus 24:10-16

The religious leaders sought to bring this charge against Jesus!

"5 When Jesus saw their faith, He said to the paralytic, "Son, your sins are forgiven you." 6 And some of the scribes were sitting there and reasoning in their hearts, 7 "Why does this Man speak blasphemies like this? Who can forgive sins but God alone?" Mark 2:5-7

But the truth is, they were blaspheming by rejecting the Messiah, and presenting a bad testimony among the Gentiles, as they themselves broke God's Law.

"For "the name of God is blasphemed among the Gentiles because of you," as it is written." Romans 2:24

The Antichrist will one day in the future blaspheme God.

"4 So they worshiped the dragon who gave authority to the beast; and they worshiped the beast, saying, "Who is like the beast? Who is able to make war with him?" 5 And he was given a mouth speaking great things and blasphemies, and he was given authority to continue for forty-two months. 6 Then he opened his mouth in blasphemy against God, to blaspheme His name, His tabernacle, and those who dwell in heaven."
Revelation 13:4-6

THE *CONFUSION*

of dignitaries - majesties (NAS); glorious ones (ESV); celestial beings (NIV); δόξα doxa noun, it means "Glory, splendor, radiance, fame, renown, honor." The question is who are these dignitaries?

"10 and especially those who walk according to the flesh in the lust of uncleanness and despise authority. They are presumptuous, self-willed. They are not afraid to speak evil of dignitaries, 11 whereas angels, who are greater in power and might, do not bring a reviling accusation against them before the Lord." 2 Peter 2:10-11

- Church leaders?
  Green, "Biggs is probably right to prefer the interpretation that it refers to church leaders, against whom the false teachers were insubordinate. The rulers of the church would naturally rebuke the false teachers, and these would naturally reply in unmeasured language."

- Angels? If so, are they good or evil angles?
  Simon Kistemaker, "Are these 'celestial beings' good or evil angels? The answer lies in the Greek word doxas

(glories) that is translated 'celestial beings' (NIV). This term accurately describes the angels that surround God's throne but does not apply to evil angels. Only God's faithful angels reflect his glory. The New Testament also teaches that the law of God "was put into effect through angels (Ac.7:53; also see v. 38; Gal. 3:19/ Heb.2:2). That is, at the time God gave the law to the Israelites, angels were His messengers. Why are these godless men slandering angels? In their desire for complete freedom, the infidels slandered angels and refused to accept the authority of anyone connected with the law." [New Testament Commentary]

Another notes, "They speak evil of dignities [doxai]. This clearly means, as in 2 Pet. 2:10, "angelic beings"; the allusion of the subsequent verse confirms the fact. It is more difficult to decide whether good or bad angels are intended. It would be most natural to suppose the former; the angels would be called doxai, because they are, as it were, rays of the Glory which is Jesus Himself. The false teachers would thus be guilty of irreverence towards God's messengers, the angels, just as the men of Sodom had been towards the angels who visited them." [Tyndale, N.T. Commentaries].

Why were the angels receiving scorn from these false teachers?

Some have suggested that the opponents were Gnostics who criticized the angels for their part in the creation of the material world.

Others think the angels were criticized as mediators of the law of Moses, which these false teachers scorned: "What purpose then does the law serve? It was added because of transgressions, till the Seed should come to whom the promise was made; and it was appointed through angels by the hand of a mediator." Galatians 3:19

Another possibility is that angels were reviled because they would play a major role on the day of judgment.

THE *CONTRAST*

[9] *But Michael the archangel, when he disputed with the devil and argued about the body of Moses, did not dare pronounce against him a railing judgment, but said, "The Lord rebuke you!"* - we know nothing about this from the

Old Testament.

We know that when Moses died God saw to his burial.

"5 So Moses the servant of the LORD died there in the land of Moab, according to the word of the LORD. 6 And He buried him in a valley in the land of Moab, opposite Beth Peor; but no one knows his grave to this day.' Deuteronomy 34:5-6

Apparently Michael had a part in this burial, at which time Satan tried to take Moses body! We are not told why Satan wanted the body, but it was probably to use it as an object of worship for Israel? Philips, "We have ample illustrations in the history of the church of the worship of relics. Deluded and gullible people will accept any bit or piece of the supposed body of a saint as having magical powers if it is properly venerated and adored. That the relic is often not even genuine makes no difference as long as the superstitious worshipers can be persuaded that it is. Emperor Leo III made strenuous and determined attempts to eradicate the worship of graven images from the church in the face of fierce opposition from pope, prelate, priest, and people alike (about a.d. 726). He had yet to learn the pride and power of the pontiffs and the religious attachment of the people to their idols. Pope Gregory III was zealous for the worship of images. He and his colleagues framed the following decree: "If any person should hereafter in contempt of the ancient and faithful customs of all Christians, and of the apostolic Church in particular, stand forth as a destroyer, defamer, or blasphemer of the sacred images of our God and Lord Jesus Christ, and of His mother, the immaculate ever-Virgin Mary, of the blessed apostles, and all other saints, he be excluded from the body and blood of the Lord and from the communion of the universal Church."...If people can be persuaded to crawl and grovel, weep and worship, plead and pray before any old, moldering piece of a corpse, Satan is delighted. The people are duped, God is mocked, and Satan laughs at the abysmal folly of unregenerate man." [John Phillip]

Truth is we do not really know why Satan wanted Moses body! It does not really matter because that is not the point Jude is making. McShane gives a good balance, "We might well ask: What claim had Satan on the body of Moses, or for that matter, on any human body? It would appear from the wording here that Satan claimed to have a legal right to the body...Obviously he was opposed to the secret burial of it, most likely because the Israelites would have embalmed it and turned it into an object of worship. However, we must give them credit, for not making the bones of Joseph an idol...We must leave the matter there, and concentrate our attention on the main reason for this reference to the body of Moses which is to demonstrate how respectful even the archangel Michael was when in dispute with Satan, yet he refused to exercise either his strength or his speech to belittle him, but left the matter in the Lord's hand, and said "The Lord rebuke you." You see a similar response in Zech. 3:2:

"1 Then he showed me Joshua the high priest standing before the Angel of the LORD, and Satan standing at his right hand to oppose him. 2 And the LORD said to Satan, "The LORD rebuke you, Satan! The LORD who has chosen Jerusalem rebuke you! Is this not a brand plucked from the fire?" Zechariah 3:1-2

We are to respect those higher than us, even those unworthy of respect like the Devil! David, for example, always treated King Saul as "the Lord's anointed," and while Saul had been publicly rejected by the Lord, David still related to him with respect. These preachers on TV that publicly rail against the Devil and arrogantly call him names, are not acting in wisdom! In the next verse Michael did not take upon himself to pass judgment on the devil but entreated the Lord to judge him. Yet the intruders in Jude community felt no compunction about reviling angelic beings. Blasphemous words whether against God or angels or God's delegated authority is foolish if not dangerous! Jude illustrated the depth of their arrogance by pointing to an encounter between the two highest angels, Michael the archangel and the devil himself. The name of Michael, the chief angel, means "Who is like God?" He has the task of opposing Satan and defending Israel (Daniel 10:13, 21; 12:1; Revelation 12:7-9). Satan began his career as perhaps the highest of all angels (cf. Isaiah 14:12-20).

"7 And war broke out in heaven: Michael and his angels fought with the dragon; and the dragon and his angels fought, 8 but they did not prevail, nor was a place found for them in heaven any longer. 9 So the great dragon was cast out, that serpent of old, called the Devil and Satan, who deceives the whole world; he was cast to the earth, and his angels were cast out with him." Revelation 12:7-9

And he is Israel's prince:

"19 And he said, "O man greatly beloved, fear not! Peace be to you; be strong, yes, be strong!" So when he spoke to me I was strengthened, and said, "Let my lord speak, for you have strengthened me." 20 Then he said, "Do you know why I have come to you? And now I must return to fight with the prince of Persia; and when I have gone forth, indeed the prince of Greece will come. 21 But I will tell you what is noted in the Scripture of Truth. (No one upholds me against these, except Michael your prince." Daniel 10:19-21

At that time Michael shall stand up, The great prince who stands watch over the sons of your people; And there shall be a time of trouble, Such as never was since there was a nation, Even to that time. And at that time your people shall be delivered, everyone who is found written in the book." Daniel 12:1

Again the main Point is that despite his high rank, Michael did not dare lay down a condemnation using blasphemous or slanderous words. Instead, he merely replied that God himself would rebuke Satan. The apostates' slandering of celestial beings (v. 8) stands in arrogant contrast to the chief angelic being, Michael, who would not dare slander Satan, chief of the fallen angels.

Swindoll, "Even the archangel Michael did not dare speak out against Satan, the leader of evil angels. But these men, the apostates, speak indignantly of divine things, charging in boldly where angels fear to tread. One characteristic of apostates is their cynical irreverence toward things that are sacred and holy."

THEIR *CONFINEMENT*

[10] But these men revile the things which they do not understand; and the things which they know by instinct, like unreasoning animals, by these things they are destroyed.

They were locked into the sense realm!

Epistantai is the knowledge that comes through instinct or the five senses; it is no better than the capacity of an animal. These men only understood their own physical lusts, and they were headed for ruin as a result of indulging those desires. These men were a clear example of the saying, "A little knowledge is a dangerous thing." The only dependable knowledge is that which comes from God's Word.

McShane, "Not being spiritual themselves they cannot possibly understand the spiritual realm and should have been content to let the unseen and unknown powers alone, but they prefer to display their hatred toward them in the most unreasonable manner, so they are not only ignorant, but malicious...There is a sphere with which they were fully acquainted, namely the flesh. Their natural instinct enabled them to know this realm apart from any schooling...Their knowledge failed to preserve from corruption or to enable them to rise above the brute beast which also has fleshly desires. It is expected that man, made in the image of God, will be respectful of his body and not allow it to be the instrument to fulfill unlawful lusts. These men, however, knew nothing about restraint, but were abandoned to the gratification of their beastly passions, and in so doing, brought about the inevitable result - their own destruction."

The Bible often compares and warns man against being compared to beasts:

"But Jeshurun grew fat and kicked; You grew fat, you grew thick, You are obese! Then he forsook God who made him, And scornfully esteemed the Rock of his salvation. Deuteronomy 32:15

The metaphor of an animal kicking at its owner:

"Do not be like the horse or like the mule,

Which have no understanding, Which must be harnessed with bit and bridle, Else they will not come near you." Psalm 32:9

"A wild donkey used to the wilderness, That sniffs at the wind in her desire; In her time of mating, who can turn her away? All those who seek her will not weary themselves; In her month they will find her." Jeremiah 2:24

Jeremiah was saying that Judah was acting like a wild animal in heat!

THEIR *CONCEIT*

Their *Source – following after their own lusts...*

Their *Speech* – they are complaining and complementing.

16 These are grumblers, finding fault, following after their *own* lusts; they speak arrogantly, flattering people for the sake of *gaining an* advantage. Jude 1:16

The Word's of these false teachers, they revealed a corrupt heart. The problem is not with our words but our heart - and the heart cannot be changed either by Law or by ignoring the law. Rabbi Joseph Telushkin proposed an annual "Speak No Evil" Day. It started on May 14, 1966. Sen. Connie Mack and Joseph Lieberman introduced a bipartisan resolution in the U.S. Senate that required the co-sponsorship of 50 senators. The resolution would establish such a day, requesting that the President issue a proclamation calling on the American people to:

- Eliminate all hurtful and unfair talk for 24 hours;
- Transmit negative information only when necessary;
- Monitor and regulate how they speak to others;
- Strive to keep anger under control;
- To argue fairly, and not allow disputes to degenerate into name-calling.
- Speak with others with the same kindness and fairness that they wish others to exercise when speaking about them.

Did it work? Hardly! All the resolutions in the world will not change the human heart. But the gospel of Jesus Christ will.

FALSE TEACHERS *WOES*

Richard Bauckham, "Whereas in vv.5-10 Jude portrayed the false teachers simply as sinners, in vv. 11-13 he portrays them as false teachers who lead other people into sin." It is one thing to be a private sinner, but much worse to be a promoter of sin to others. Continuing with the Depiction of the false teachers, we have seen their world and words and now their Woes (Jude 11)

Woe to them - The interjection ouai is found over 60 times in the Septuagint to express a variety of related emotions. It translates hôy, 'ôy, and occasionally 'î, hôwafah, and hî. These all derive from roots meaning "to howl"

Kistemaker, "The lamentation Woe to them, is a typical phrase that the O.T. prophets uttered repeatedly to condemn persons or nations. Jesus uses the word woe to place a curse on Korazin and Bethsaida (Mt.11:21), and He rebukes the Pharisees with a series of seven woes (Mt. 23). And Paul calls a woe upon himself should he fail to preach the gospel (1Cor.9:16). Likewise, Jude pronounces woes upon his godless contemporaries and tells them that they are heading for destruction. At the same time his words are a warning to his readers not to permit these godless men to lead them astray."

THE *ROAD* OF CAIN

For they have gone in the way of Cain - the

first son of Adam and Eve, born outside of Eden. I believe that the way of Cain—is that they promote a religion of works without faith (Gen. 4:3-8; Heb. 11:4/ 1Jn.3:12).

Wuest, "Woe" is ouai, "an interjection of grief or of denunciation," here, the latter. "Way" is hodos, "a road, a way," metaphorically, "a course of conduct, a way, manner of thinking, feeling, deciding."

The Scofield Bible speaks of Cain as the "type of a religious, natural man who believes in a God and in 'religion,' but after his own will, and who rejects redemption by blood. Compelled as a teacher of religion to explain the atonement, the apostate teacher explains it away." "Gone" is poreuomai, "to take one's way, set out, to go on a journey," metaphorically, "to follow one, to become his adherent."

"1 Now Adam knew Eve his wife, and she conceived and bore Cain, and said, "I have acquired a man from the LORD." 2 Then she bore again, this time his brother Abel. Now Abel was a keeper of sheep, but Cain was a tiller of the ground. 3 And in the process of time it came to pass that Cain brought an offering of the fruit of the ground to the LORD. 4 Abel also brought of the firstborn of his flock and of their fat. And the LORD respected Abel and his offering, 5 but He did not respect Cain and his offering. And Cain was very angry, and his countenance fell. 6 So the LORD said to Cain, "Why are you angry? And why has your countenance fallen? 7 If you do well, will you not be accepted? And if, you do not do well, sin lies at the door. And its desire is for you, but you should rule over it." Genesis 4:1-7

"By faith Abel offered to God a more excellent sacrifice than Cain, through which he obtained witness that he was righteous, God testifying of his gifts; and through it he being dead still speaks. Hebrews 11:4

Cain was no *Different* than Abel

- By *Birth* - they were both born sinners. Rom.5:12
  Mackintosh, "Cain and Able were born, not inside, but outside of paradise - they were the sons, not of innocence, but of fallen Adam. They came into the world, as the partakers of the nature of their father; and it mattered not in what way, that nature might display itself, it was sinful nature still - fallen, ruined depraved nature." Psa.51:5; 58:3

- By *Behavior* - both committed acts of sin. Rom.3:23/Gal.3:22

- *Both Believed* in something - both had faith!
  Cain's faith was demonstrated by bringing an offering to God - he was not an atheist. Most American's believe in God - so do demons! Ja.2:19
  Cain had faith in what he brought - or he would not have brought it. Problem faith is only as good as its object. All faith in the world will not allow a busted chair to hold you up. The difference was not in them; in themselves both were helpless and hopeless sinners.

Cain alone was *Disobedient*

- A God-given *Obligation* - either instructed by God or by Adam and Eve that fig leaves were a no-no, but it must be a figurative lamb (Gen.3:15). Heb. 11:4 makes it clear that Abel offered by faith, which presupposes revelation (Rom.10:17). MacDonald, "There must have been a time when Cain and Able were instructed that sinful man can approach the holy God only on the ground of the blood of a substitutionary sacrifice. Cain rejected this revelation and came with a bloodless offering of fruits and vegetables."

- The only God-given *Object* - a bloody substitute.
  Seen in the many individual lambs offered by Job, Abraham, etc; in the Passover lamb; in the lamb offered on the Day of Atonement; in Jn.1:29.
  Principle" Jn.14:6
  Sanders, "Faith does not exist apart from the object on which it is focused. And the object which faith relies, is not our faith, but that which enables us to see. Our responsibility is not to concentrate on our faith, but on God. Jesus alone is the sinners' Savior, faith simply looks to Him.

Therefore Cain's religion was *Deficient*

No blood! That is why Able offered to God a more excellent sacrifice then Cain. (Heb.11:4) See, Heb.9:22. Religion seeks to give something to God; Righteousness comes from receiving everything from God...

Cain's religion was *Defiant*, in that he knew better!

His heart was not right - "not as Cain who was of the wicked one and murdered his brother. And why did he murder him? Because his works were evil and his brother's righteous." (1 John 3:12). Even the right sacrifice, from the wrong heart will not be accepted - the Pharisees offered the prescribed sacrifices.

"The sacrifice of the wicked is an abomination; How much more when he brings it with wicked intent!" Proverbs 21:27

"23 Now when He was in Jerusalem at the Passover, during the feast, many believed in His name when they saw the signs which He did. 24 But Jesus did not commit Himself to them, because He knew all men, 25 and had no need that anyone should testify of man, for He knew what was in man." John 2:23-25

His wicked heart was soon manifested in murdering his brother Abel. Wiersbe, "Cain rebelled against God's way of salvation, by clothing Adam and Eve with the skins of slain animals (Gen. 3:21), God made it clear that the only way of forgiveness is through the shedding of blood. This is the way of faith, not the way of good works (Eph. 2:8-10). But Cain rejected this divinely authorized way and came to the altar with the fruits of his own labor.

God rejected Cain's offering because God rejected Cain: his heart was not right before God. It was by faith that Abel's sacrifice was offered, and that was why God accepted it (Heb. 11:4). The "way of Cain" is the way of religion without faith, righteousness based on character and good works. The "way of Cain" is the way of pride, a man establishing his own righteousness and rejecting the righteousness of God that comes through faith in Christ (Rom. 10:1-4; Phil. 3:3-12). Cain became a fugitive and tried to overcome his wretchedness by building a city and developing a civilization (Gen. 4:9ff). He ended up with everything a man could desire, everything except God, that is. "Nobody is more furious than an apostate after hearing a good sermon on the blood! The Bible places the utmost of importance upon the shed Blood of Christ.

'In whom we have redemption through his blood, even the forgiveness of sins." (Colossians 1:14)

"But now in Christ Jesus you who sometimes were far off are made nigh by the blood of Christ." (Ephesians 2:13)

"For the life of the flesh is in the blood: and I have given it to you upon the altar to make an atonement for your souls: for it is the blood that makes an atonement for the soul." (Leviticus 17:11)

Of sin the Bible says, "Without the shedding of blood is no remission. (Hebrews 9:22)

On the cross Christ shed his blood to pay the ransom and set us free from the chains of bondage that enslave the human race. Jesus said, If the Son therefore shall make you free, ye shall be free indeed. (John 8:36) The only way to be saved and set free from the power of sin is by the blood of Christ. Yet, Cain would not accept it; neither will the apostates." [Expository Pulpit Series]

Feeling Forgiven? Someone asked Martin Luther, "Do you feel that you have been forgiven?" He answered, "No! But I'm as sure as there's a God in heaven. For feelings come and feelings go, and feelings are deceiving; My warrant is the Word of God, nought else is worth believing. Though all my heart should feel condemned for want of some sweet token, There is One greater than my heart, whose Word cannot be broken. I'll trust in God's unchanging Word, till soul and body sever; For though all things shall pass away, His Word shall stand forever."

McGee, ""Woe unto them!" The word for "woe" is the Greek word ouai. The very pronunciation of this word is a wail -- "Ouai, ouai!" It denotes a wail of grief or of denunciation. Here it is more a wail of denunciation, but it is both. Of these apostates whom Jude has just identified, he now says, "Woe unto them!" "For they have gone in the way of Cain." Cain was a religious man but a natural man. He believed in God and believed in religion, but he did it after his own will. He denied that he was a sinner, rejected redemption by blood, and thought that he could come his own way to God. Hebrews 11:4 certainly tells the story: "By faith Abel offered unto God a more excellent sacrifice than Cain, by which he obtained witness that he was righteous, God testifying of his gifts: and by it he being dead yet speaketh." Cain is dead also, yet he speaks. The way of Cain is the way of a man who refused to bring a little lamb which pointed to Christ. In other words, Cain did not come to God by faith. He did not believe God when He said that man was to bring a little lamb for a sacrifice, that without shedding of blood there is no forgiveness of sins, and that the penalty must be paid. Cain thought that he could come to God his own way, and that is the picture of the apostate today. The apostate calls himself a liberal and a modernist; but, my friend, this is as old as the Garden of Eden. Right outside the Garden of Eden, Cain was a modernist and a liberal. He believed in religion and God, but he did it his own way, not God's way."

God's way is through the substitutionary death of Christ.

Dennis Fulton, former pilot with the Wings of Caring ministry in Zaire, tells of landing a newly purchased Cessna 402 at one of his regular stops in the back country. As always, the villagers excitedly gathered around the plane, but this time Dennis was approached by two men carrying a live chicken. One had the bird by the feet, and the other had it by the head, and before either the chicken or Dennis knew what was happening, the fowl's head and body parted company. The man with the flopping chicken corpse began swinging it over his head, round and round, with predictable results. Dressed in a freshly pressed white shirt, Dennis was splattered with chicken blood, as were the plane and the villagers. When Dennis asked what that meant, a native explained that for generations, the splattered blood had signified an end to suffering. To the people of Zaire, the Cessna promised hope and help of all kinds. In a graphic way, the splattered blood of that chicken, signifying the end of suffering, was a fitting reminder of the blood Christ shed to end the suffering of a world caught in the grip of sin. The Road of Cain leads to hell! It is coming to God our way instead of God's way. His way is always and only through the substitutionary death of Christ. Kaisertal, Austria is a remote Alpine village. It is one of the last inhabited valleys in the Alps not connected by a road to the outside world. In this isolated mountain village, food and fuel are carried in on an aerial ropeway. Its few vehicles were winched up the stairs long ago and are now stranded there, in an Arcadian landscape of fields and farm-houses, encircled by jagged, snow-capped peaks. There is archeological evidence that Kaisertal has been inhabited for thousands of years. For the current 30 people who live in Kaisertal, there has always been one way in and one way out: on foot. There are 236 wooden steps on a footpath that winds up the steep slope to Kaisertal. For those residents who need medical help or food, or just want to go and see a movie, there is only one way. They must put on their hiking boots and hike the 236 steps of the footpath to reach the outside world. Jesus Christ is the only way to God. We all must put our faith in Him to receive eternal life.

REWARD OF BALAAM

Leo Tolstoy, the famous Russian writer, had a deep insight into human nature. In one of his books he speaks of a Russian peasant who was told that he could have all the land he could measure by walking in one day, from sunrise to sunset. The agreement stipulated that by sundown he must be back at his starting point. The man envisioned great holdings. Early in the morning he began walking; but as he realized that every foot of land on which he stepped belonged to him, he began to run at a feverish pace. The agreement stipulated that by sundown he must have returned to his starting point. His greed was so great, however, that more than half his time had elapsed before he turned back. He had to run at top speed to beat the setting sun. It was a real struggle. If he were not at the appointed place, he would lose all. He finally made it. But even as his foot touched the starting point, he fell dead from exhaustion. All that he gained in the end was sufficient land for his dead body—six feet of earth.

We continue looking at the Woe's of false teachers, we saw the Road of Cain; now the Reward of Balaam.

and for pay they have rushed headlong into the error of Balaam -

THE *ANALYSIS* OF OUR PASSAGE

rushed headlong - The idea here is, that all restraint was relaxed, and that they rushed on tumultuously to any course of life that promised gain. It appears 10 times in the New Testament primarily denoting "to pour out." Three of these passages are located in the account of the Last Supper in which Jesus explained to His disciples how His blood would be "poured out" or "shed" for many (Matthew 26:28; Mark 14:24; Luke 22:20). The same word is used to refer to the blood of martyrs being "poured out" (Matthew 23:35; Luke 11:50). Ekchunō is also employed in relation to Judas' death (Acts 1:18), to the "pouring out" of the Holy Spirit on the Gentiles (Acts 10:45), to the vastness of the love of God (Romans 5:5), and in our passage to godless men running "greedily . . . for reward" (Jude 11).

Woe upon them!...like Balaam, they will do anything for money;"   Jude 1:11 (TLB)

These people will do anything for money! "What are you willing to do for $10,000,000? Two-thirds of Americans polled would agree to at least one, some to several of the following: Would abandon their entire family (25%) Would abandon their church (25%) Would become prostitutes for a week or more (23%) Would give up their American citizenship (16%) Would leave their spouses (16%) Would withhold testimony and let a murderer go free (10%) Would kill a stranger (7%) Would put their children up for adoption (3%)."

into the error of Balaam - the idea is wandering (from the path of truth); error, delusion. Planē, "error," stands over against the truth of the gospel, and it threatens those unstable in their faith:

"that we should no longer be children, tossed to and fro and carried about with every wind of doctrine, by the trickery of men, in the cunning craftiness of deceitful [plane] plotting," Ephesians 4:14

"17 You therefore, beloved, since you know this beforehand, beware lest you also fall from your own steadfastness, being led away with the error of the wicked; 18 but grow in the grace and knowledge of our Lord and Savior Jesus Christ. To Him be the glory both now and forever. Amen." 2 Peter 3:17-18

"Deception" is a trick employed by religious hucksters who sell religion for profit. This is not a tactic used by the preacher of the gospel who speaks frankly and honestly on the basis of Scripture:

"2 But even after we had suffered before and were spitefully treated at Philippi, as you know, we were bold in our God to speak to you the gospel of God in much conflict. 3 For our exhortation did not come from error or uncleanness, nor was it in deceit. 4 But as we have been approved by God to be entrusted with the gospel, even so we speak, not as pleasing men, but God who tests our hearts. 5 For neither at any time did we use flattering words, as you know, nor a cloak for covetousness--God is witness. 6 Nor did we seek glory from men, either from you or from others, when we might have made demands as apostles of Christ." 1 Thessalonians 2:2-6

Wiersbe, "The "way of Balaam" is merchandising one's gifts and ministry just for the purpose of making money. It is using the spiritual to gain the material (see 1 Thes. 2:5-6; 1 Tim. 6:3-21). The false teachers were greedy for material gain and, like Balaam, would do anything for money. The "error of Balaam" is thinking that they can get away with this kind of rebellion. Balaam was a true prophet of God, but he prostituted his gifts."

for profit - Payment, wages, reward, punishment. Misthos is used most often in the New Testament in a figurative and eschatological sense. In the Sermon on the Mount Jesus exhorted His disciples to rejoice in their earthly persecution for they, like the prophets, would receive their "reward" in heaven (Matthew 5:12; Luke 6:23). Likewise the believer's stewardship and sacrificial life-style on earth will be rewarded in heaven (Matthew 5:46; 6:1, 2, 5, 16; cf. Luke 6:35). Those who support the work of Christ by supporting His disciples will also have a share in the heavenly "reward."

40 "He who receives you receives Me, and he who receives Me receives Him who sent Me. 41 He who receives a prophet in the name of a prophet shall receive a prophet's reward. And he who receives a righteous man in the name of a righteous man shall receive a righteous man's reward. 42 And whoever gives one of these little ones only a cup of cold water in the name of a disciple, assuredly, I say to you, he shall by no means lose his reward." Matthew 10:40-42

Paul reminded the Corinthians that "every man shall receive his own reward according to his own labor" (1 Corinthians 3:8; cf. 3:14; Revelation 11:18). Every person will receive a "reward" after his life on earth is done; however, not every "reward" will be desirable. There is the "reward of iniquity:

Now this man purchased a field with the wages of iniquity; and falling headlong, he burst open in the middle and all his entrails gushed out. Acts 1:18

There is the "wages of unrighteousness" (2 Peter 2:13, 15).

"13 and will receive the wages of unrighteousness, as those who count it pleasure to carouse in the daytime. They are spots and blemishes, carousing in their own deceptions while they feast with you, 14 having eyes full of adultery and that cannot cease from sin, enticing unstable souls. They have a heart trained in covetous practices, and are accursed children. 15 They have forsaken the right way and gone astray, following the way of Balaam the son of Beor, who loved the wages of unrighteousness;" 2 Peter 2:13-15

It was Jesus who made the final appeal for urgency and integrity in the believer's earthly work when He said, "And, behold, I come quickly; and my reward is with me, to give to every man according as his work shall be" (Revelation 22:12). So there are "rewards" for both the good and the evil (e.g., Matthew 6:19, 20; 19:21; Romans 2:5, 6). Note: The Bible is clear that there is a valid supporting of God's teachers:

"11 If we have sown spiritual things for you, is it a great thing if we reap your material things? 12 If others are partakers of this right over you, are we not even more? Nevertheless we have not used this right, but endure all things lest we hinder the gospel of Christ. 13 Do you not know that those who minister the holy things eat of the things of the temple, and those who serve at the altar partake of the offerings of the altar? 14 Even so the Lord has commanded that those who preach the gospel should live from the gospel."
1 Corinthians 9:11-14

But the motive is never to make money! Paul testified, "I have coveted no one's silver or gold or apparel." Acts 20:33

"Shepherd the flock of God which is among you, serving as overseers, not by compulsion but willingly, not for dishonest gain but eagerly;" 1 Pet. 5:2

"Jude saw a parallel between Balaam and the opponents, for like Balaam "they poured themselves out" ("have rushed," NIV) for the sake of money. The parallel with Balaam suggests that the opponents were false teachers, probably wandering prophets who spoke to make money. The error of Balaam relates to his teaching. The active sense is nicely captured by Louw and Nida, "They gave themselves completely to the kind of deception that Balaam practiced for the sake of money." In their teaching the opponents propagated error in order to make money, and yet at the same time they were deceived enough to believe their own error. Some have said that the error the teachers "rushed" into was sexual sin, but it does not make sense to say that they committed sexual sin for the

sake of money. It probably is the case, however, that their teaching included the idea of sexual license." [New American Commentary]

Nelson study Bible, "Balaam epitomized the sin of greed. He was a pagan prophet, an enemy of God, who believed he could profit from doing the work of God. Similar to Balaam, the ungodly teachers in the church appear to be religious. They sought to mix in with the people of God, and they were even accepted by the believers. However, their true motive was greed."

THE HISTORICAL *ACCOUNT*

The OT shows Balaam as an instrument of blessing in Num. 22-24 and of seduction and consequent immorality and apostasy in Num. 31:16:

I. First, a curse Sought. 22:1-30
A. Balak's Worry. 22:1-4
It was not justified, God had instructed them to leave the Moabites alone (Deut. 2:9).
B. Balak's Wish. 5-7
That was an impossibility (Gen. 12:1-3).
C. Balak's Worldliness. 8
His motive was greed. 2 Pet. 2:12-17
D. God's Warning. 9-12
Richards, "God clearly told Balaam, "Do not go with them." This was God's directive will, what He had instructed Balaam to do. But Balaam pursued to see "what else" God would say on the matter. The problem is that Balaam sought to change God's mind. He knew God's will, but he did not want to obey it."
E. Princes of Moab Withdraw. 13-14
F. Balak's Wealth. 15-17
G. Balaam's Wrong. 18-19
H. God's Wrath. 20-40
1. A Limitation. 20-21
Go, but not as a loose cannon...

2. A Lesson - God confirms the limitation.
We must remember God looks at people's heart, and Balaam's heart was greedy, he wanted to find a way to curse Israel so he could get the money. This donkey had more discernment then Balaam! Somebody asked D.L. Moody if he really believed that a donkey spoke to Balaam. Moody replied, "Oh yes. That is not hard to believe. In fact you make a donkey and I will make it speak!" The God who can do the greater, create the donkey, can surely do the lesser, make him speak!
II. Furthermore a blessing wrought. 22:41-24:25
A. First Prophecy: A Chosen people. 22:41-23:12
B. Second Prophecy: An unbeatable Champion. 23:13-26
C. Third Prophecy: A Choice land to dwell. 23:27-24:14, v. 5
D. Fourth Prophecy: The Christ is coming. 24:15-25, v.17
III. FINALLY A COMPROMISE TAUGHT. 25:1-18; 31:16
A. The Decadence. 25:1-3
1. Sexual Immorality. 25:1
2. Idolatry. 2-3
B. The Dis-allowance. 4
Moses put a stop to it!
C. The Defiance. 6, 14-15
D. The Deliverance. 7-15
E. The Disturbance. 16-18

The Reward of Balaam is choosing money over the masters will. This reminded me of Yussif, the Terrible Turk! Yussif was the 350 pound wrestling champion in Europe a little over two generations ago. After he won the European championship, he sailed to the United States to beat our champ, whose name was Strangles Lewis-- a little guy, by comparison, who weighed just a shade over two hundred pounds. Although he wasn't huge, Strangler had a simple plan for defeating his opponents. It had never failed to work. He'd put that massive arm of his around the neck of his opponent. He'd pump up that bicep and cut the oxygen off, right up there near the Adam's apple. Many an opponent had passed out in the ring with Strangler Lewis. The problem he had when it came to fighting the Turk was that the European giant didn't have a neck! His body just went from his head to those massive shoulders. Lewis could never get the hold, so it wasn't long before Yussif flipped Lewis down on the mat and pinned him. After winning the championship, the Turk demanded all 5,000 dollars in gold. After he wrapped the championship belt around his vast middle, he stuffed the gold into the belt and boarded the next ship back to Europe. He was now the possessor of America's glory and gold. He set sail on the SS Bourgogne . Halfway across the Atlantic, a storm struck and the ship began to sink. Yussif went over the side with his gold still strapped around his body. The added weight was too much for the Turk, and he sank like an iron anvil before they could get to him with the lifeboats He was never seen again. That's the way of these false teachers - they are motivated by sheer greed and yet none of their wealth will help them in the Day of Judgment.

THE *REBELLION* OF KORAH

Malcolm Muggeridge had an interview with Svetlana Stalin, the daughter of Josef Stalin. She spent some time with Muggeridge in his home in England while they were working together on their BBC production on the life of her father. According to her, as Stalin lay dying, plagued with terrifying hallucinations, he suddenly sat halfway up in bed, clenched his fist toward the heavens once more, fell back upon his pillow, and was dead.
The incredible irony of his whole life is that at one time Josef Stalin had been a seminary student, preparing for the ministry. But he made a decisive break from his belief in God. And as Stalin lay dying, his one last gesture was a clenched fist toward God, his heart as cold and hard as steel. False teacher's stubbornness is ultimately met with the Woe of judgment.
We continue with a Depiction of the false teachers - their World, Words, and Woes - the

woe of the Road of Cain; the Rewards of Balaam; and now the Rebellion of Korah.

AN *ANALSIS* OF THE PASSAGE

and perished - the verb means to Destroy, ruin, kill, lose, be lost, perish, to put to death. It is used of ruined wine skins (Luke 5:37). The word focuses on loss of well-being and describes the eternal woeful condition of the lost in the hereafter.

in the rebellion of Korah - Korah was a Levite, a member of the tribe set apart by God to minister to the spiritual needs of Old Testament Israel, both in the wilderness and, later, in the land. He was a cousin of Moses and Aaron (Exod. 6:18-21). Jude accuses him of "rebellion" The Greek work is antilogia, meaning "to contradict." The word pictures vigorous opposition, possibly opposition by act as well as word. The word is used to describe the opposition that Jesus faced and overcame: "Consider him that endured such contradiction [antilogia] of sinners against himself" (Heb. 12:3). The word can be translated "strife." In the Septuagint, in five places where the Hebrew has "Meribah," the translators use the Greek word antilogia (Num. 20:13, 27:14; Deut. 32:51, 33:8; Ps. 81:7). Korah was the one who led a mutinous mob against Moses.

And like Cain and Balaam before him, he was a teacher. His distinguishing mark of instruction was his disdain for the Biblical notion of authority. We read about this in Numbers 16:1-4:

"1 Now Korah the son of Izhar, the son of Kohath, the son of Levi, with Dathan and Abiram the sons of Eliab, and On the son of Peleth, sons of Reuben, took men; 2 and they rose up before Moses with some of the children of Israel, two hundred and fifty leaders of the congregation, representatives of the congregation, men of renown. 3 They gathered together against Moses and Aaron, and said to them, "You take too much upon yourselves, for all the congregation is holy, every one of them, and the LORD is among them. Why then do you exalt yourselves above the assembly of the LORD?" 4 So when Moses heard it, he fell on his face; Numbers 16:1-4

It is like one taking the truth about the priesthood of all believers and interpreting it to remove any notion of authority. Korah is unhappy living under the authority of another.

THE HISTORICAL *ACCOUNT* See, Num. 16.

AN *ACCURATE* LOOK AT REBELLION

Special Study on Rebellion:

I. *Cases* of Rebellion Found in the Bible.

- Lucifer—He wanted to exalt his throne above God.
- Cain—He offered a bloodless sacrifice to God.
- Samson—He disobeyed God and his parents by playing with sin and the wrong crowd.
- Absalom—He rebelled against his father and attempted to overthrow his kingdom permanently.
- Hophni and Phineas—The sons of Eli lived a wicked life and committed sin at the temple of the Lord.
- The Sons of Korah—They rebelled against Moses' leadership and authority.
- Jonah—He ran from God when he was called to serve.
- Israel—They rebelled against God seven times in the book of Judges.
- Achan—He took the garment, gold, and silver which was a direct violation of God's command.
- The Prodigal Son—He rebelled against the teachings of his father.

- Saul—He did not destroy Agag and the sheep as commanded.

II. Bible *Comments* on Rebellion:

- Deuteronomy 31:27—Stiffed neck
- 1 Samuel 15:23—Rebellion is as the sin of witchcraft.
- Psalm 68:6—The rebellious dwell in a dry land.
- Isaiah 30:1—The rebellious cover their sin and do not take counsel of God.
- Isaiah 65:2, 5—They walk in their own thought and have a holier than thou attitude.
- Ezekiel 12:2—They see not and hear not.
- Zechariah 7:12—They made their heart as an adamant stone.

III. The *Catastrophe* of Rebellion:

- Lucifer—He and his followers were cast out of heaven.
- Cain—Cain was cursed.
- Samson—He lost his strength for service, his eyes, strength, and life.
- Absalom—He lost his life.
- Sons of Korah—They were swallowed up into the earth.
- Jonah—A great whale swallowed him

- Israel—They were chastised by their enemies, went into captivity.
- Achan—Achan lost his family and his life.
- Prodigal son—he wasted his inheritance.

IV. The *Consequences of* Rebellion:

- Robs you of God's blessings.
- Ruins your testimony for Jesus Christ.
- Makes our hearts Receptive for sinful pleasures.
- Releases God's just judgment.
- Rewards you with misery and unhappiness.
- Reduces your ability to discern spiritual truths from God's Word.
- Relaxes your attitude towards praying and Bible study.
- Replaces God's authority with self or Satanic authority.

V. The *Cure* For Rebellion:

- Repentance
- Revealing—We are to confess our sin to the Lord and make things right with one another. 1 John 1:9
- Replacement—Replace bad habits with good habits.

- Request—Request prayer, counsel, and help.
- Refrain—Refrain from sinful pleasures, temptations, wrong crowds.
- Refuge—Get alone with the Lord each day.
- Remember—Remember the misery we bring upon ourselves and others when we rebel.

The Woes - whether it is the Road of Cain, or the Reward of Balaam, or the Rebellion of Korah, or these false teachers, all of their works and words will ultimately be destroyed in judgment. After spending months writing his book, The French Revolution, Thomas Carlyle took his manuscript to his friend John Stuart Mill for his comments. Mill passed the manuscript on to a lady named Mrs. Chapman, who read it by the fireplace on the evening of March 5, 1834. Before she went to bed that night she laid the manuscript on the mantel. Early the next morning the servant girl came to clean the room and to start the fire in the fireplace. Not knowing what the papers were, the servant used the manuscript as fuel to kindle the fire. The work of months was burned up in a matter of seconds.

FALSE TEACHERS *WAYS*

Five iceberg warnings were telegraphed to the ill-fated Titanic. When the sixth message, "Look out for icebergs," came in, the Titanic operator wired back: "Shut up, I'm busy." Exactly 35 minutes later the great ship was sinking. The warnings against the danger of ungodly false teachers, usually goes unheeded, but the danger is just as real. We are still looking at the Depiction of the ungodly false teachers, we have seen their World; Words; and Woes, now their ways. We will see that they are like Submerged Rocks; Lying Skies; insufficient Soil; roaring Sea; and wandering Stars.

12 These are the men who are hidden reefs in your love feasts when they feast with you without fear, caring for themselves; clouds without water, carried along by winds; autumn trees without fruit, doubly dead, uprooted; 13 wild waves of the sea, casting up their own shame like foam; wandering stars, for whom the black darkness has been reserved forever. Jude 1:12-13

THEY ARE LIKE *SUNKEN [SUBMERGED]* ROCKS

These are the men who are hidden reefs in your love feasts when they feast with you without fear, caring for themselves...

They are *Dangerous*

hidden reefs - This noun appears once in the New Testament (Jude 12) where there is considerable debate about its meaning. Primarily the debate is whether Jude 12 used it to mean "spot, stain" or a "dangerous rock, reef." The greater part of classical usage would call for the meaning "rock over which the sea dashes," although it can also denote a "slab" or other exposed, land-based rock (Liddell-Scott). Except for Jude 12 there is but one instance of the word referring to a "spot" in Greek literature—in a Fourth Century A.D. document. Not only does this fit the most well-attested usage of the word, it also "makes excellent sense. In context the word should indicate the danger which the false teachers present to Jude's readers...(They) are like dangerous reefs; close contact with them will result in shipwreck" (ibid.). This means the false teachers were like submerged rocks, unseen by sailors, that could wreck a ship.

McGee, "An apostate may be compared to the tip of an iceberg. Very little of it is visible, but if a ship runs into it, the ship will go to the bottom of the sea. Oh, how many people there are especially young people, whose faith has not only been shaken but wrecked by a person who is an apostate?"

According to the Associated Press, on December 14, 1996, a 763-foot grain freighter, the Bright Field, was heading down the Mississippi at New Orleans, Louisiana, when it lost control, veered toward the shore, and crashed into a riverside shopping mall. At the time the Riverwalk Mall was crowded with some 1,000 shoppers, and 116 people were injured. The impact of the freighter demolished parts of the wharf, which is the site of two hundred shops and restaurants as well as the adjoining Hilton Hotel. An apt example of the damage false teachers can cause in the spiritual realm.

"19 having faith and a good conscience, which some having rejected, concerning the faith have suffered shipwreck, 20 of whom are Hymenaeus and Alexander, whom I delivered to Satan that they may learn not to blaspheme." 1 Timothy 1:19-20

They are *Deceptive*

in your love feasts, while they feast with you -
they are right there in the local church! Notice
it is not the preaching of the Word, but the
feasting on food that attracts them! Table
fellowship was far more significant among the
ancients and the Orientals than it is among
modern Westerners. In older times, in Eastern
lands, to sit at table with someone implied a
bond of friendship and fellowship. Some
cultures still consider "a covenant of salt" to
be sacred. Orientals would not break bread
with someone whom they intended to
betray. The treachery of Ahithophel was made
all the worse, in David's eyes, because David
often had entertained him at his table (1
Chron. 27:33-34; Ps. 41:9). The same was
true of Judas Iscariot. The sin of the apostates
is aggravated by the fact that they use every
means at their disposal to profess oneness
with the establishment that they are actually
undermining and betraying. In Jude's day,
they continued to seek oneness with true
believers by a show of hearty good fellowship
at the love feasts of the early church. [John
Phillips Commentary Series]

We have to watch out for deception!

"Do not be deceived: "Evil company corrupts good habits." 1 Corinthians 15:33

"6 Let no one deceive you with empty words, for because of these things the wrath of God comes upon the sons of disobedience. 7 Therefore do not be partakers with them." Ephesians 5:6-7

"Little children, let no one deceive you. He who practices righteousness is righteous, just as He is righteous." 1 John 3:7

And yet such deception exists...

Spurgeon, "We must expect to find ungodly men in the Christian Church. They ought not to be there: the church is bound to use her most earnest endeavors to keep them out and, being in and being discovered, she should not be slow to cast them forth. She should put away wicked members and endeavor to preserve her purity; but for all that, there will never be a perfect church this side of the grave. A mixed multitude always will be mingled with [God's people] while we are in this wilderness. Our Lord had but twelve disciples who were near to him, and yet he said, "I have chosen you twelve, and one of you is a devil." The name of Judas will go down to eternity stamped with the curse, "It were better for that man that he had never been born." Look again at the church in Samaria. The preaching of Philip had stirred the city, and a pretender to magic who had deluded the people, professed to become himself a believer. He believed, it is said, and was baptized; but his heart was not right in the sight of God: his faith was not the faith of God's elect. How solemn were the words of Peter to him, "Thou hast neither part nor lot in this matter...For I perceive that thou art in the gall of bitterness, and in the bonds of iniquity!" The execrable name of Simon Magus is another proof that the church of Christ in her most zealous estate, cannot expect to be clear of the basest of men. Our own observation and the history of any branch of the Lord's church will go to show the same thing. It is said that the emperor Frederick III, once heard a courtier declare that he would go forthwith to a place where he should find no hypocrites. Then, said his majesty, "You had need to go beyond the frozen ocean, where there are no men; and if you should reach the place, there might be one hypocrite there then."

They are *Dauntless* [Invulnerable to fear or intimidation]

without fear - Fearlessly, without fear, boldly. There is arrogance about the ungodly but it is a false confidence. "God Himself could not sink this ship," boasted a deckhand aboard R. M. S. Titanic in 1912. The men who built the ship, the civilized world, the credulous public—all believed and boasted that the ship was unsinkable.

They are Self *Directing*?

caring for themselves - has the idea to herd or tend sheep; rule, govern; shepherd, care for, look after, nourish. The words here reflect Ezek 34:2: "Woe to the shepherds of Israel who only take care of themselves! Should not shepherds take care of the flock?" Or, as Ezek 34:8 says, "My shepherds did not search for my flock but cared for themselves rather than for my flock." The reference to shepherds indicates that the opponents were leaders, claiming that they had the ability to guide and lead God's people. But they had no concern for anyone but themselves. The way a true shepherd feeds the sheep is by the Word of God, but these men only belittle God's Word and thus have no real food to give anyone. How many preachers today are nothing more than self-serving proclaiming anything but the clear uncompromising Word of God?

Marvin Gardiner wrote the twentieth-century novel, The Flight of Peter Fromm. Set on the streets of Hyde Park, within the shadow of the University of Chicago, the book traces the disheartening journey of one young man, Peter Fromm, from his belief in the gospel to something else, a faith more suitable for his enlightened age. At one point in the narrative, the young man's mentor schools his student on the makeup of a good preacher. "To be a minister today in the typical church of a prosperous suburb, one must be as skilled as a politician in the rhetoric of ambiguity, circumlocution, and double talk. He must talk plain language though in such a way that no listener can take offense. He may attack race prejudice, but it must be done obliquely so that no one in the congregation imagines that it refers to him. He may attack business ethics, but it must be done in such a manner that no businessman who listens will think that he is implicated. Today's preacher can indeed use all doctrinal phrases but always so cunningly that conservative listeners will take them one way, liberal listeners another.
In brief he must learn to preach without saying anything."

Their way is that of sunken rock which cause shipwrecks. But we can be those of a different sort! Lutzer shared about, The Witness of John Harper:

"Let me take you back in time; the date is Wednesday, April 10, 1912, and the world watches in awe as the glamorous Titanic begins her maiden voyage. But, little did the world know that the greatest ship man ever made would be on the bottom of the Atlantic ocean only four days later. And on that ship, in the second-class section, was a man named John Harper who was coming to America to preach here at Moody Church. I first heard the phenomenal story of John Harper, many years ago while growing up in Canada. My brother showed me a one-page tract titled I was Harper's Last Convert. It was the story, told by a man, who floated next to Harper briefly in the icy waters of the Atlantic. If you had been with John Harper on the Titanic that fateful night you would have felt a tremendous jolt when the mighty ship collided with an iceberg on the starboard side of her bow. You would have heard the hull plates buckle as an iceberg tore a 300-foot long gash in the side of the ship. And you may have even heard the panic in the Captain's voice when he knew his ship was sinking, and he only had enough lifeboats for half of the passengers....The Captain also knew he had to keep order among the 2,227 people on board. So he asked John Harper to remain on deck and keep peace among the passengers. If you had been on deck you would have seen families torn apart. Husbands saying goodbye as they watched their wives and children leave on lifeboats. Wives deciding to stay on board to die with their husbands. Children waving goodbye to their parents—and praying that they would see each other again. And you would have seen John Harper kiss his six-year-old daughter, Nana, goodbye and put her safely in a lifeboat. As the minutes crept by, and all of the lifeboats were gone, 1,521 people were left on board the sinking ship—including Harper. With every minute that passed the deck became steeper as the bow plunged under the water. Finally the ship broke in two, hurling the remaining passengers into the icy depths of the Atlantic. It is said the ships lights blinked once, then went out, leaving people to freeze to death in the darkness of the Atlantic. And the few hundred people that were safe in lifeboats could see their husbands, fathers, and many other families as they were shrieking in terror and thrashing in the water trying to gasp for breath. But, during this horrific tragedy God was at work. You see, Harper wasn't afraid to die; he knew that he was going to come face to face with his Maker. And he wanted other people to know his Lord and Savior.

Though his later exploits are not certain, it has been reported that Harper gave his lifebelt to another man before he went down with the ship. One survivor tells of finding himself, with hundreds of others, "struggling in the cold, dark waters of the Atlantic." He said, "I caught hold of something and clung to it for dear life, the wail of the perishing all around was ringing in my ears." A stranger drifted near him and encouraged him to look to Jesus for his soul's safety. The two drifted apart and then together again. The stranger, floating alongside in the 28-degree waters, encouraged him again to call out to Jesus. As they drifted apart, the stranger could be hard making his same plea to others struggling in the moonless night. So with death lurking over him, Harper yelled to a man in the darkness, "Are you saved?" "No," replied the man. "Believe on the Lord Jesus Christ and ye shall be saved!" Harper screamed as he struggled in the dark, cold, Atlantic. Then the men drifted apart into the darkness. But later the current brought them back together. Weak, exhausted, and frozen, a dying Harper yelled once more, "Are you saved?" "No!" Harper repeated once again, "Believe on the Lord Jesus Christ and ye shall be saved." And with that, Harper slipped down into his watery grave. "Then and there, with two miles of water beneath me, in my desperation I cried to Christ to save me." The man whom Harper sought to win to Christ was rescued by the S.S. Carpathia, and he lived to tell people that he was Harper's Last Convert."

Of course in reality he wasn't John Haper's convert at all, he was the convert of Jesus Christ.

THEY ARE LIKE LYING *SKIES*

Swindoll, "Viewed together these vivid pictures bring to life the character sketch of these false teachers. They are as deceptive as hidden reefs; as disappointing as clouds without water; as dead as trees that are without fruit and uprooted; as destructive as wild waves of the sea, and as doomed as falling stars."

We continue looking at the Depiction of these false teachers - looking at their Ways we observed that they were like Submerged rocks which caused shipwreck; and now we see they are like.

They are *Promising*

clouds without water - First; let's look at what the Bible says about clouds. Rarely do clouds appear in the Bible in a simple meteorological context, but the limited references to clouds and weather reveal that the Hebrews were careful observers of nature. Elijah's servant knew that a cloud rising from the sea meant rain:

"Then it came to pass the seventh time, that he said, "There is a cloud, as small as a man's hand, rising out of the sea!" So he said, "Go up, say to Ahab, 'Prepare your chariot, and go down before the rain stops you.'" 1 Kings 18:44

The very first mention of clouds comes after the flood where God establishes a new relationship with humankind through Noah, symbolized by a rainbow in the clouds (Gen 9:12-17). After the exodus from Egypt, when the Israelites wander in the wilderness for forty years, their journey is marked by a pillar of cloud by day and a pillar of fire by night (Ex 13:21, 22; 14:19, 20, 24, see later reflections in Neh. 9:12, 19; Ps 78:14; 99:7; 105:39; and 1 Cor. 10:1-2). Exodus 16:10 associates the cloud in the wilderness with the "glory of the Lord." The cloud and the fire represent God's presence with them during their sojourn. The cloud represents God's presence but also his hiddenness. No one can see God and live, so the cloud shields people from actually seeing the form of God. It reveals God but also preserves the mystery that surrounds

him. During their wilderness wanderings, the Israelites camp for a long time at the foot of Mount Sinai. While there, God reveals himself and his law to Moses and the people on top of the mountain. As the people look at the mountain, they hear and see "thunder and lightning, with a thick cloud over the mountain" (Ex 19:16 NIV, cf. also 24:16, 18; 34:5). Once again God's appearance is marked by cloud. Also in the wilderness, God instructs the Israelites to build a place where they might worship him. We know this mobile sanctuary as the tabernacle or tent of meeting. God makes his presence known there by means of a cloud that fills the most holy part of the building (Ex 33:9, 10; 40:34-38; Lev 16:2; Num 9:15-23). When the temple later replaces the tabernacle as the place where God makes his presence known to Israel, that building too is filled with the cloud of God's glory (1 Kings 8:10-11; 2 Chron 5:13-14). Centuries later, when God turns against Israel because of its sin, he abandons his temple. Ezekiel sees this as the departure of the cloud from the Holy of Holies (Ezek 10:3-4). A number of passages associate God's appearance as a warrior with the cloud. Isaiah looks into the future and sees God moving in judgment against Egypt:
See, the Lord rides on a swift cloud
and is coming to Egypt. The idols of Egypt

tremble before him, and the hearts of the Egyptians melt within them. (Is 19:1-2 NIV) While biblical writers associate clouds primarily with the appearance of God, they occasionally reveal other aspects: They can illustrate the transience of life: "As the cloud disappears and vanishes away, So he who goes down to the grave does not come up." Job 7:9 of God's grace, blotting out human sin: "I have blotted out, like a thick cloud, your transgressions, And like a cloud, your sins. Return to Me, for I have redeemed you." Isaiah 44:22 [Dictionary of Biblical Imagery]

In our passage the picture is of a farmer who is experiencing a drought; he desperately needs rain to save his crop. He looks over the horizon and sees clouds gathering. This gives the promise of rain. False teachers come with great promises...These men had no water for thirsty souls; they only pretended that they did. And they were soon gone, unstable as wind-driven clouds.

McGee, "Clouds they are without water." They may look as if they are filled with the Word of God, but they are empty and dry. They may wear robes and speak in pompous, pontifical voices with great authority. They have had courses in public speaking and homiletics, and they know how to spiritualize a text of

Scripture and make it mean something entirely different from what God intended. They are like beautiful clouds that drift across the sky without giving any refreshment to the earth. There was no water in them at all. Well, that is Jude's picture of apostates. They do not have the water of life. They actually know nothing about the Word of God."

False promises are pie crust promises, in the movie Mary Poppins, the two children, Jane and Michael Banks, jumped into bed after their incredible first day with the amazing Mary Poppins. Jane asked, "Mary Poppins, you won't ever leave us, will you?" Michael, full of excitement, looked at his new nanny and added, "Will you stay if we promise to be good?" Mary looked at the two and as she tucked them in replied, "Look, that's a pie-crust promise. Easily made, easily broken!

They are *Disappointing*

carried along by the winds - in other words those clouds which promise rain, and blown away by a strong wind thus blowing away the hope of needed rain. The image of the wind is intended to portray the unreliability of human teaching in contrast to the truth of faith:

"that we should no longer be children, tossed

to and fro and carried about with every wind of doctrine, by the trickery of men, in the cunning craftiness of deceitful plotting," Ephesians 4:14

"What an fitting picture of the false teacher! The idea here is of a drought stricken land, the drought has taken its toll on the crop. The sun is blistering hot, and the ground is dry and cracked. The time is critical, without rain the crops will soon be dead and all lost. Then yonder in the distance, clouds begin to form and roll in over the fields. What a sight! Rain at last! But hours later the clouds have cleared and there is still no rain. That is a picture of false teachers and apostates. Carried about by every wind of doctrine and wickedness, they appear to be genuine but after all is said and done, there is nothing but hot air; the water of life has been withheld." [Expository Pulpit Series]

"Do not be carried about with various and strange doctrines. For it is good that the heart be established by grace, not with foods which have not profited those who have been occupied with them." Hebrews 13:9

False teachers cannot fulfill their promise...

"Like billowing clouds that bring no rain is the person who talks big but never produces." Proverbs 25:14 (MSG)

"Palestine is a dry climate, tremendously dependent upon rains at crucial times to sustain life. When rain is desperately needed and thick clouds appear, the anticipation of and hope for rain climaxes. If no rain falls, bitter disappointment ensues. The opponents were like such clouds. They promised much but delivered little." [New American Commentary]

Philips, "The apostates are disappointing. They are "clouds without water, carried about by winds." The picture is that of a dry and thirsty land longing for rain. The earth is baked as hard as iron and the sky gleams like burnished brass. Dust blows across the land. It piles upon the alleys and drifts in through windows and doors. It settles on floors and furniture. It blankets fences. It settles on drooping bushes and trees and chokes the life out of once hopeful crops. Even the weeds succumb. Then hope gleams in every eye and beats anew in every breast; there is a cloud in the sky! It seems to be a very angel of God. It grows and spreads, and its welcome shade brings cooling and promise to the parched soil. Men pray, cattle lift their weary heads, and the shriveled flowers yearn for rain. But the cloud is a cheat, a heartless sham. It gathers its fleecy folds about itself and drifts away on the wind as the triumphant sun resumes its relentless reign over the drought-stricken land. Have pity on the people in the pew who trust such deceptive pastors in the pulpit. They seem to have such promise. They sound so convincing. They seem to say what they are supposed to say. Like clouds in the sky, they seem so far above the ordinary, unsuspecting people who come to their churches or enroll in their seminaries. Often, they are witty and eloquent and quote the Bible. No matter that they substitute reason for revelation, psychology for Holy Spirit conviction, good works for saving faith, a mutilated Bible for an inspired, inerrant, infallible Scripture. The thirsty people who look eagerly to them for that life-giving revival shower look to them in vain. They have nothing, so can give nothing, to bring life to a dying world."

In March 1997 police came to a Rancho Santa Fe, California, mansion and found the corpses of thirty-nine people who had said yes to the wrong thing. They were members of the Heaven's Gate cult, impressionable people who had left homes, friends, and families all across America to follow cult leader Marshall

Applewhite. The police found their bodies clothed in black and shrouded in purple. They had committed mass suicide, believing that their souls would leave their bodies and join up with a spaceship that they hoped was trailing behind a comet passing near earth. A false teacher can be compared to a slot machine—offering lots of promise but rarely delivering the goods. Every day people gamble with their money, hoping finally to "hit the jackpot." But they seldom do. Instead, the gambler continues to insert his quarters and pull the handle waiting for something that will never come. Ray was a young man who was hooked on "one-armed bandits" (a popular slot machine). He lived each day in hopes of finally hitting the big one. It got so bad for him that he began to fall into debt because of his habit. "Just one more quarter," was his argument. "I can walk away any time I wish." Ray had no idea how addicted he was, but his father did. It took some time, but Ray was able to get some help from Gamblers Anonymous. False teachers lure people in with their lies and their promises. But they are filled with emptiness and instability. They are totally untrustworthy. Like the slot machine, they promise something that will never happen. And poor souls like Ray have to deal with the consequences. Don't waste your time on a false teacher. You are gambling with your life if you do. [Teacher's Outline and Study Bible]

God's Word is like clouds that produce needed rain!

"1 "Give ear, O heavens, and I will speak; And hear, O earth, the words of my mouth. 2 Let my teaching drop as the rain, My speech distill as the dew, As raindrops on the tender herb, And as showers on the grass." Deuteronomy 32:1-2

"9 "For as the heavens are higher than the earth, So are My ways higher than your ways, And My thoughts than your thoughts. 10 "For as the rain comes down, and the snow from heaven, And do not return there, But water the earth, And make it bring forth and bud, That it may give seed to the sower And bread to the eater," Isaiah 55:9-10

Spurgeon commenting on that verse, "If you believe this great promise, you shall have the full benefit of it. Let this gracious rain drop on you, and it must refresh you. Let these blessed snowflakes some down on you, and they shall melt into your bosom, and remain there to bless you forever; they shall not go back to God with their mission unfulfilled. As for us who preach that Word, or teach it in the

Sunday-school, we may have a full assurance that we shall not labor in vain nor spend our strength for naught. No, no; the raindrops go not on an errand that can fail, and the snowflakes that fall to the earth accomplish the end for which they are sent. Much more shall the purpose of God's Word be accomplished! Behold, it drops like the gentle rain; like snowflakes fly the messages of mercy from the lips of the Lord himself, and they shall not fall in vain, blessed be his holy name!"

A promise from God is a statement we can depend on with absolute confidence. Here are 12 promises for the Christian to claim:

- God's *Presence* - "I will never leave you" (Heb. 13:5)
- God's *Protection* - "I am your shield" (Gen. 15:1)
- God's *Power* - "I will strengthen you" (Isa. 41:10)
- God's *Provision* - "I will help you" (Isa. 41:10)
- God's *Pioneering* - "And when He puts forth His own sheep, He goes before them" (John 10:4)
- God's *Purposes* - "I know the thoughts that I think toward you, says the Lord,

thoughts of peace, and not of evil"
(Jer. 20:11)

- God's *Pillow* - "Come unto Me, all ye
  that labor and are heavy laden, and I
  will give you rest" (Matt. 11:28)
- God's *Purifying* -"If we confess our
  sins, He is faithful and just to forgive
  us our sins, and to cleanse us from all
  unrighteousness" (1 John 1:9)
- God's *Pleasantry* - "No good thing will
  He withhold from them that work
  uprightly" (Psalm 84:11)
- God's *Promptness* - "The Lord will not
  forsake His people for His great name's
  sake" (1 Sam. 12:22)
- God's *Pointing* -- "The meek will He
  guide" (Psalm 25:9)
- God's wise *Plan* - "All things work
  together for good to them that love
  God" (Rom. 8:28)

What a contrast between God's promises and
mans! My estate consists principally of my
books. I have a little house and property in
Decatur, but that is really the banks. But
suppose when my heirs gather to listen to the
reading of my will, they hear, "I leave to my
son Jeremy a yacht in the Gulf of Mexico; I
leave to my daughter Missi one hundred acres
in Florida; I leave to my son and daughter all
the mineral rights that I hold in Nevada, to be

divided among them." You know what would happen, don't you? My children would say in sympathy, "Poor Dad! He must have been mentally deranged to write a will like that! It is a meaningless will because he owned none of those things. He cannot make good on that will!" But when Bill Gates dies and leaves a will to his heirs, everyone listens closely for his or her own name because this is a will with resources behind it. Just so, faith does not rest merely on promises. It goes back to the character of the One who makes the promises. So is we are wise we will turn a deaf ear to the promises of the apostates and stand firmly on the promises of God, found in His Word.
"Behold, this day I am going the way of all the earth. And you know in all your hearts and in all your souls that not one thing has failed of all the good things which the LORD your God spoke concerning you. All have come to pass for you; not one word of them has failed." Joshua 23:14

THEY ARE LIKE *STONE-DEAD* TREES

Dr. Walter Wilson, tells of how he was called to conduct a funeral service. The day of the funeral was rainy and the roads were muddy, so he asked the undertaker if he could ride with him. As the two were riding along the preacher asked the undertaker whether he ever read in the Bible the verse that says, "Let the dead bury their dead." He winced and said, Come on preacher, there is no such passage in the Bible. That wouldn't make any sense. How can a dead person bury another dead person?" Walter said, "Oh it's in there! Those words were spoken by the Lord Jesus himself. You say that you are not a Christian, so you are a dead undertaker in front of this hearse, driving out to the cemetery to bury this dead friend in the back of the hearse. That friend is dead to his family and you are dead to God. He does not respond to them; neither do you respond God." These false teachers were just as dead!

They were *Unfruitful*

autumn trees without fruit - They were like trees "without fruit" in the late autumn when fruit was expected. Autumn is the season when farmers and gardeners expect to harvest the final crops of the year. It was late autumn and the tree still had not borne any fruit. Some trees may bear their fruit late, but the time for waiting had passed, and now the hope for any fruit was extinguished.

"This is a picture of false teachers offering hope to people, but their hope is empty and unstable—just as empty and unstable as the hope of these unfruitful trees. The false teachers cannot water the seed of God's Word in people's hearts, nor can their teaching bear fruit within people. The opinions of false teachers cannot help people in facing the trials and temptations of life, nor can they prepare people to face eternity that lies just over the horizon. In dealing with eternity—with God, Christ, and the Holy Scripture—the false teacher is nothing more than...a tree without fruit. He may sound like he offers hope, security, and fullness of life; but his message is unstable and empty and will leave a person hopeless when he meets God face to face." [Teacher's Outline and Study Bible - Commentary]

"When a wicked man dies, his expectation will perish, and the hope of the unjust perishes." Proverbs 11:7

What a contrast with the Christian hope!

"The hope of the righteous will be gladness, but the expectation of the wicked will perish." Proverbs 10:28

One of my favorite hymns:

My Hope is built on nothing less,
Then Jesus blood and righteousness,

I dare not trust the sweetest frame
But wholly lean on Jesus name.

On Christ the solid rock I stand
All other ground is sinking sand,
All other ground is sinking sand.

We Christians have:

- The Hope laid up in heaven for us (Col. 1:5).
- Jesus as our "Our Hope" (1 Tim. 1:1).
- A Hope that purifies us (1 Jn. 3:3).
- A hope based on the gospel (Col. 1:23).
- This hope is part of our armor (1 Thess. 5:8).
- It is the hope [expectation] that we will be righteous in our very experience (Gal. 5:5).
- Hope that we will live forever and ever and ever in eternal bliss (Tit. 3:7).
- Hope is part of the Christians calling (Rom. 8:24-25/ Eph.1:18/Eph.4:4).
- Our hope is Christ eternally in us (Col. 1:26-27).
- This hope can never die (1 Pet. 1:3).
- The very rapture we look for is a hope (Tit. 2:13).

They were also Unfruitful because they were separated from Christ!

"4 Abide in Me, and I in you. As the branch cannot bear fruit of itself, unless it abides in the vine, neither can you, unless you abide in Me. 5 I am the vine, you are the branches. He who abides in Me, and I in him, bears much fruit; for without Me you can do nothing." John 15:4-5

McShane, "There is only one purpose for fruit trees and that is that they bear fruit; if they fail in this then they are useless and must be rooted up."

What is real fruit?

- Character (Gal. 5:22-23).
- Godly Conduct (Col. 1:10).
- Converts (Rom. 1:13/ 1 Cor. 16:15).
- Communication of praise to God (Heb. 13:15-16)
- Contributions (Rom. 15:26-28/Phil. 4:14-17).

According to Julie Iovine in the New York Times, in the 1990s many owners of small farms in America began to reduce their wholesale farming to a mere sideline and instead started using their property for another purpose: entertainment farming. "Entertainment farmers attract paying customers to their property with country bands, hay-bale mazes, petting corrals, and tricycle courses. City-dwelling families eager for a feel of life on the farm can pay $12 for admission, food, and amusements. It can cost a child $1 to frolic in a pile of straw or pick a flower. Some farms have mazes cut into their cornfields that can take a person forty-five minutes to navigate. Iovine reports that one farmer in Arizona makes up to $15,000 on a good weekend. In 1994 Alaska and Oklahoma introduced entertainment farming as official parts of their state tourism policies. The catalyst for many of these farmers to take up agritainment was economic pressure.

These false teachers resemble an entertainment farmer. They produce no spiritual fruit, but entertain their followers with carnal eternally unproductive things.

They were *Uprooted*

they were doubly dead, uprooted - Verb, part. aor. pass voice, lit "having been rooted up." In saying that they were "twice dead," he is using an expression that is an emphatic way of saying they were "totally dead." In the original "uprooted" follows "twice dead." Jude may have been saying, then, that they were dead in that they bore no fruit, and they were also dead because they had been pulled up from the ground. No one, of course, expects fruit from uprooted trees.

"12 Then His disciples came and said to Him, "Do You know that the Pharisees were offended when they heard this saying?" 13 But He answered and said, "Every plant which My heavenly Father has not planted will be uprooted."

McShane, "When trees are said to be "twice dead," they are worse than fruitless, for a tree may be barren one year, and bear fruit the next, but dead trees could never become fruitful. Viewed in the winter, fruit trees have the appearance of being dead, but when spring time comes, they [come back to life], no so, with twice dead trees! They not only appear to be dead in the dead of winter, but are dead in spring. They will never live again."

So it is with these false teachers, they have firmly rejected Jesus Christ and so there is no hope for such people! Mr. Tabor is famous in Colorado history. He was a successful mining man, having made millions from his "Matchless mine" near Cripple Creek,

Colorado. He divorced his wife that he might marry the beautiful divorcee, Baby Doe. This illicit marriage became one of the outstanding social events of the early West. The President of the United States was invited to the wedding—and he came.

But soon misfortune overtook them, and Mr. Tabor lost his money. He died a broken-hearted and a poor man. Just before his death he gave "Baby Doe" this final admonition: "Have faith in the Matchless mine; never give it up; it will give you back all that I have lost." Baby Doe, the now forlorn and aging widow, took him at his word. She lived near, and guarded the Matchless mine for the next 36 years of her desolate life, and stayed near the mine, in the face of repeated court ousters and crushing adversity. In 1935 she died in a dilapidated shack near the mine, her hopes never realized. Her life was a dismal failure and she came to a sad end because she put hope and faith in the wrong object. The false teachers may look hopeful for a time, but the truth is in the end they, and their followers, will end up in a hopeless eternity! So they are Stone-dead as uprooted trees.

History and the Bible make it clear; there is no hope for those who reject the gospel of Jesus Christ.

Henry Kissinger said: "I think of myself as a

historian more than a statesman. As a historian, you have to be conscious of the fact that every civilization that has ever existed has ultimately failed. "History is a tale of efforts that failed, of aspirations that weren't realized, of wishes that were fulfilled and then turned out to be different from what was expected. "So, as a historian, one has to live with a sense of the inevitability of tragedy. As a statesman, one has to act on the assumption that problems can be solved."

THEY ARE LIKE A *SAVAGE STORM*

"But the wicked are like the troubled sea, when it cannot rest, whose waters cast up mire and dirt." (Isaiah 57:20)

Butler notes, "Scripture never describes the wicked in a way that would make the righteous look inferior. Sometimes to the human eye, it seems that the wicked prosper while the righteous suffer. But to the spiritual eye, this apparent contradiction is just that— apparent. The righteous are the ones who have it best. When life is over and eternity is in view, this fact will be very evident to all. Isaiah shows that the wicked lack peace, power, and purity.

- Lack of peace. "The wicked are like the troubled sea." Here the wicked is described as a troubled sea. It is a sea in turmoil. There is no peace. The waves are tossed about in a tempest. Sin kills peace. It is why the world is always at war. Sin does not bring peace to any land or soul. It only troubles the land and the soul of man. The wicked put up a front of confidence and assurance, but inside they are greatly disturbed. This world has rejected Christ and, as a result, knows nothing but war! A former president of the Norwegian Academy of Sciences and historians from England, Egypt, Germany, and India has come up with some startling information: Since 3600 B.C. the world has known only 292 years of peace! During this period there have been 14,351 wars, large and small, in which 3.64 billion people have been killed. The value of the property destroyed would pay for a golden belt around the world 97.2 miles wide and 33 feet thick. Since 650 B.C. there have also been 1656 arms races, only 16 of which have not ended in war. The remainder ended in the economic collapse of the countries involved.

- Lack of power. "When it cannot rest." Sin overpowers the sinner. Sin makes the sinner weak. He does not have the power to overcome evil habits. The sinner "cannot" stop the turmoil that comes to his life because of sin. He is helpless, He loses control of his life and cannot gain control back because he lacks that power. Sin enslaves man, and he becomes a servant of sin. Only through redemption in Christ Jesus does man gain back that power to overcome evil and get free from the bondage of sin. Again the wicked give the outward impression of being in control and demonstrating great power, but the reality is of an inner weakness.

- Lack of purity. "Whose waters cast up mire and dirt." The wicked are foul and filthy. Like the wild waves of the sea which throw dirt and mire on the shore, the wicked are always throwing up filth wherever they are. Their mouths continually spew out dirt. Their minds think dirt, and their deeds are dirty. But Christ is the answer here. His blood can cleanse the sinner from sin and make him clean before God.

Jude continues on with by depicting the way of the false teacher is like a Savage Storm. They are like Submerged rocks; lying Skies; Stone-dead trees; and now they are likened to a Savage Storm.

Their *Prideful boasts*

 wild waves of the sea, casting up their own shame like foam -"In classical Greek agrios primarily denotes "wild, savage, or living in the fields." It occasionally is used as an adverb in the form of agriōs meaning "savagely." It is when agrios is used in its primary form as an adjective of either animals or trees and is translated "wild," or when it is employed to describe circumstances and is translated "stormy, wild," that it relates closest to the New Testament use." Agrios appears only three times in the New Testament and in two different contexts. In the occasions where it is found in the Gospels, it is used of the honey that John the Baptist ate and denotes "wild" or "found in an open field" (Matthew 3:4; Mark 1:6). In Jude 13 it is employed with waves as a metaphor and is rendered "stormy" or "raging to the point of foaming," emphasizing the turbulence and general state of unsettledness of godless men."

waves - is used literally of the "waves" of the Sea of Galilee (Matthew 8:24; 14:24; Mark 4:37) and of the Mediterranean Sea (Acts 27:41). It is related to the verb kuō which means "to swell" or "to be pregnant." Kuma was used figuratively in classical Greek of men who were tossed about by their passions (cf. Liddell-Scott). Jude used this language metaphorically to describe apostates." Jude compared the apostates to "raging waves of the sea" not because of their power, but because of their pride and arrogant speech. "Their mouth speaks great swelling words" (Jude 16). Like a violent storm, they make a lot of noise! To people who kept criticizing his administration, President Lincoln once told the following story:

"A traveler on the frontier found himself, as night came on, in a wild region. A terrible thunderstorm added to his trouble. He floundered along until his horse gave out and then had to get out to lead him. Occasional flashes of lightning afforded the only clue to the path, and the crashes of thunder were frightful. One bolt, which seemed to crush the earth beneath him, made him stagger and brought him to his knees. Being by no means a praying man, his petition was short and to the point: 'Oh Lord! If it's all the same to you, give us a little more light and a little less noise!' The root problem is pride! An article titled "The Art of Being a Big Shot" was written by a very prominent Christian businessman named Howard Butt. Among many other insightful things he said were these words:

It is my pride that makes me independent of God. It's appealing to me to feel that I am the master of my fate, that I run my own life, call my own shots, go it alone. But that feeling is my basic dishonesty. I can't go it alone. I have to get help from other people, and I can't ultimately rely on myself. I'm dependent on God for my next breath. It is dishonest of me to pretend that I'm anything but a man— small, weak, and limited. So, living independent of God is self-delusion. It is not just a matter of pride being an unfortunate little trait and humility being an attractive little virtue; it's my inner psychological integrity that's at stake. When I am conceited, I am lying to myself about what I am. I am pretending to be God, and not man. My pride is the idolatrous worship of myself. And that is the national religion of Hell! [from an undocumented source].

That false teachers in reality worship themselves, pretending to be God, is the pride that cause their destruction.

What they *Produce*

Nothing of *Substance*

Just foam! - "This is a symbol of the lightness, frivolity and worthlessness of many of earth's great men, as God viewed their lives. Jude 13. This type describes the expressions of the ungodly in word and action. They make a great noise and a great appearance, and then subside into silence and oblivion." [A Dictionary of Bible Types]

casting up their own shame like foam - The waves are lashed into foam, and break and dash on the shore. They seem to produce nothing but foam, and to proclaim their own shame, that after all their wild roaring and agitation they should effect no more. So it is with, these noisy and vaunting teachers. What they impart is as unsubstantial and valueless as the foam of the ocean waves, and the result is in fact a proclamation of their own shame, Men with so loud professions should produce much more." [Notes on the New Testament Explanatory and Practical].
When all is said and done they produce nothing of worth!

John Calvin, "Why this was added, we may

learn more fully from the words of Peter: [2 Peter 2:17-18] it was to shew, that being inflated with pride, they breathed out, or rather cast out the scum of high-flown stuff of words in grand eloquent style. At the same time they brought forth nothing spiritual, their object being on the contrary to make men as stupid as brute animals. You may justly say that they make only rumbling sounds; They seem at one time to carry their disciples above heaven, then they suddenly fall down to beastly errors."

A few minutes after the elegant new $6,000,000 Pittsburgh post office was opened to the public, customers began complaining that there was no letter drop. Dismayed Postmaster Turner got in touch with the architects, who embarrassingly confessed they had actually forgotten all about the important item. The false teachers are like that...

Nothing but *Shame*

shame - speaks of something disgraceful.

"The wise shall inherit glory, But shame shall be the legacy of fools." Proverbs 3:35

"When pride comes, then comes shame; But

with the humble is wisdom." Proverbs 11:2

Tony Evans, "TWO brothers went away to college. One brother became a farmer. The other became a brilliant, wealthy lawyer. The lawyer brother visited the farmer brother on the farm. He said, "I can't believe you've not made anything of your life. You're out here on a farm. Look at me. Look where I am. I'm on Wall Street. I'm an investor in the stock market. I have clients who are millionaires. Here you are, stuck out here on the farm. I wonder what the difference between us is." The farmer brother then spoke. He pointed out to his wheat field. He said, "You'll see two types of wheat out there, brother. You'll see the wheat that's standing straight up. In the head of that wheat, there is nothing. It's empty. That's why it's standing so high. You'll also see some other wheat that is bent over. That's because the head is full. It's full of wheat." Some of us are standing straight up. We are walking tall. However, we are only able to do so because we are empty. Some of us walk a little bent over indicating that we are full. The test isn't what you have in your pocket. It's what you have in your heart.

"A righteous man hates lying, but a wicked man is loathsome and comes to shame." Proverbs 13:5

I read in one of those Daily Breads, "While attending college, I visited a psychiatric institution with a group of students to observe various types of mental illness. The experience proved to be very disturbing. I remember one man who was called "No Hope Carter." His was a tragic case. A victim of venereal disease, he was going through the final stages when the brain is affected. Before he began to lose his mind, this man was told by the doctors that there was no known cure for him. He begged for one ray of light in his darkness, but had been told that the disease would run its inevitable course and end in death. Gradually his brain deteriorated and he became more and more despondent. When I saw him in his small, barred room about 2 weeks before he died, he was pacing up and down in mental agony. His eyes stared blankly, and his face was drawn and ashen. Over and over he muttered these two forlorn and fateful words: "No hope! No hope!" He said nothing else."

"17 Brethren, join in following my example, and note those who so walk, as you have us for a pattern. 18 For many walk, of whom I have told you often, and now tell you even weeping, that they are the enemies of the cross of Christ: 19 whose end is destruction, whose god is their belly, and whose glory is in their shame--who set their mind on earthly things." Philippians 3:17-19

At 3 a.m. on April 5, 1956, newspaper columnist Victor Riesel walked out of Lindy's restaurant in mid-town Manhattan. In his columns Riesel had crusaded for some time against gangster infiltration and corruption of labor unions, and earlier that night he had done a radio broadcast in which he assailed the leadership of a Long Island union. Accompanied by a friend and his secretary, Riesel headed toward his car, which was parked on 51st Street. Near a theater, according to Lawrence Van Gelder in the New York Times, a young man stepped from the shadows and threw liquid into Riesel's face. It was acid. The acid hit Riesel in the eyes and blinded him. One month later doctors told Riesel he would never see again. Riesel later wrote, "There was no terror at the moment when I knew I had crossed the line into permanent darkness. There was only a sudden feeling of shame. I was afraid that people would treat me too gently or shy away from me as though from a freak. And suddenly, I wondered if I could go on writing and earning a living." These false teachers had spoken against God, and had crossed the line into permanent darkness - a darkness that would eventually cause them great shame.

Shame always comes as a result of rejecting God's Word:

"And if anyone does not obey our word in this epistle, note that person and do not keep company with him, that he may be ashamed." 2 Thessalonians 3:14

"Be diligent to present yourself approved to God, a worker who does not need to be ashamed, rightly dividing the word of truth." 2 Timothy 2:15

They are live like Savage storms! They are loud and proud but produce nothing but shame! Pali, this bull has killed me." So said Jose Cubero, one of Spain's most brilliant matadors, before he lost consciousness and died. Only 21 years old, he had been enjoying a spectacular career. However, in this l958 bullfight, Jose made a tragic mistake. He thrust his sword a final time into a bleeding, delirious bull, which then collapsed. Considering the struggle finished, Jose turned to the crowd to acknowledge the applause. The bull, however, was not dead. It rose and lunged at the unsuspecting matador, its horn piercing his back and puncturing his heart. These false teachers think they have put Jesus Christ and His truth to death, they stand loudly and proudly receiving man's applause - but they will soon learn that Jesus Christ is alive and will come to them in wrath.

LIKE *SHOOTING STARS*

When I was a kid I was into boxing. I could tell you just about anything you wanted to know about the sport. It used to infuriate my mother, "Son if you can remember all these boxing facts, why can't you remember what they tell you in school!" Anyway I remember a new upcoming boxer named Boone Kirtman, he was promoted as another Rocky Marciano, a great white hope. He turned pro sometime in the mid 1960s, and he was from Seattle. Almost all of his early fights took place on the west coast. He was supposed to be a fairly strong, hard-hitting guy in the style of Bonavena and Quarry. He won something like 23 of his first 24 fights, and most of the wins came by knockout. I was a convert; I knew this guy was going to be the greatest heavyweight of all time! Kirkman's big chance came when he faced a young upcoming George Foreman - I figured this would be easy pickings for Boone! Foreman destroyed Boone in only two rounds, and Boone was so discouraged he stayed out of boxing for the next two years. By and large for all the hype Boone Kirkman was merely a flash in the pan.

These false teachers were like that - merely a flash in the pan. Like Shooting Stars!

They were like a *Flash in the pan*

The Meaning of the phrase 'flash in the pan' is, "Something which disappoints by failing to deliver anything of value, despite a showy beginning." Some believe that this phrase derives from the Californian Gold Rush of the mid 19th century. Prospectors who panned for gold supposedly became excited when they saw something glint in the pan, only to have their hopes dashed when it proved not to be gold but a mere 'flash in the pan'. This ties in with another phrase related to disappointment - 'it didn't pan out'. 'Panning out' can be traced to US prospectors and was used in that context by the early 20th century. Others say, the phrase did have a literal meaning, i.e. it derives from a real flash in a real pan, but not a prospector's pan. Flintlock muskets used to have small pans to hold charges of gunpowder. An attempt to fire the musket in which the gunpowder flared up without a bullet being fired was a 'flash in the pan'. At any rate it is a perfect description of these false teachers, who had a showy beginning but would have no lasting value.

wandering - A wanderer. *star* - ἀστήρ astēr

noun astēr means "star, meteor," or "planet." Comets, meteors, and shooting stars were called "wandering stars" in the 1st century. I believe he is comparing them to shooting stars:"Wandering stars refer to the shooting stars which make a beautiful and brilliant show, but last for only a few minutes and then disappear into the darkness. This is a picture of the apostate who puts on a good show for now but will ultimately be cast into outer darkness (Matthew 25:30)" [Expository Pulpit Series]

Rienecker, "...describes shooting stars which fall out of the sky and are engulfed in darkness."

Wiersbe, "Jude was not referring to fixed stars, planets, or comets, because they have definite positions and orbits. He was referring to meteors, falling stars that suddenly appear and then vanish into the darkness, never to be seen again."

MacArthur, "Wandering stars does not refer to heavenly bodies that continuously shine and have fixed orbits. Most likely the expression signifies a meteor or "shooting star" that flashes across the sky in an uncontrolled moment of brilliance and then disappears forever into the black darkness (cf. v. 6).

Apostates often appear for a short time on the stage of Christianity. They promise enduring spiritual light and direction but deliver nothing but an erratic, aimless, worthless flash. The utter blackness and darkness of hell has been reserved forever for them (cf. 2 Peter 2:4, 9, 17)."

"Wandering stars (i.e., "shooting" stars), move across the sky, shining briefly, and then vanish without production light or giving direction. Fixed stars help guide navigators, but wandering stars are useless to them. If any shipmaster would be stupid enough to follow one, he would be led astray. Similarly the prominence of apostate leaders is short-lived, useless, and false. They do lead unwary followers astray, pretending to be what they are not. They will therefore be swallowed up into the blackest darkness forever; eternal judgment is certain for them." Reminds me of the 8 track tapes, they looked so promising but were quickly replaced by the cassette tape, which is still in use and has been for many years - yet are now being replaced by CD's.

They were to be *Forever Punished*

Their *Destiny*

reserved - Watch carefully, guard; keep, hold in reserve, preserve; observe, obey, pay attention to. Tēreō is particularly important in the New Testament and is used of keeping (i.e., obeying) the commandments (Matthew 19:17; 1 Timothy 6:14; James 2:10; cf. Revelation 12:17; 14:12). It especially refers to keeping Jesus' commands or His word—synonymous ideas (John 8:51, 52; 14:15, 21, 23, 24; 1 John 2:3-5; 5:3). Jesus himself modeled such obedience by keeping the word of the Father (John 8:55; 15:10; 17:6). Acts uses tēreō almost exclusively of imprisonment. While the believer is being kept by Jesus Christ (Jn.17:11-12, 15), these false teachers were being kept for judgment.

Their *Darkness*

black darkness - It speaks of thick gloom; darkness - σκότος skotos noun Dark, darkness, gloom. CBL, "In the New Testament skotos is used over 30 times to figuratively depict an unalterable reality. Evil is real and has power, and "darkness" is often used to depict this (Luke 22:53). All men are being influenced by the principalities, the rulers of "darkness" (Ephesians 6:12). The effects of darkness on men take different forms. In Romans 2:19 skotos is used of intellectual "darkness," but usually it refers to moral or spiritual "darkness" (Luke 1:79; 11:35; John 3:19; Acts 26:18; 2 Corinthians 6:14; Colossians 1:13; 1 Thessalonians 5:4,5; 1 Peter 2:9; and 1 John 1:6). In Matthew 6:22ff. Jesus taught that the "sound (haplous [568]) eye" permits light's entrance (phōteinos [5296]), but the "evil eye" (ponēros [4050]) makes the whole body "darkness." Here, the contrast is intentionally shown between "darkness" as evil and "sound" as light (good). In Ephesians 5:8 Paul spoke of those who were in "darkness" before but now are "light."

"Darkness" is the domain of death (Matthew 22:13; 25:30; cf. Luke 1:79) that rules the world. Darkness ruled until Jesus, but as Isaiah prophesied, "The people living in darkness have seen a great light" (Matthew 4:16, NIV; Isaiah 9:2). John particularly developed the theme that the realm of Jesus is the light, but the world and its ways are darkness (skotia, e.g., John 1:5; 8:12; 12:35). The gospel summons men and women (especially used of Gentiles in the Biblical texts) to turn from darkness and Satan's power to the light (Acts 26:18; cf. Ephesians 5:8; 6:12; Colossians 1:13; 1 Peter 2:9). Those in the light have nothing in common with those living in darkness (2 Corinthians 6:14; Ephesians 5:11; 1 Thessalonians 5:4).

Ultimately, darkness will be the punishment of the wicked, that is, separation from God (2 Peter 2:17; Jude 13), and in that place of punishment there will be "weeping and gnashing of teeth" (Matthew 8:12). But those whose names are written in the Book of Life will live where there is no "night" (Revelation 21:25; 22:5)."

Problem: Is hell a place of darkness, or is there light there? Jesus described hell as a place of "outer darkness" (Matt. 8:12; cf. 22:13 and 25:30). By contrast, the Bible says hell is a place of "fire" (Rev. 20:14) and "unquenchable flames" (Mark 9:48). But, fire and flames give off light. How can hell be utterly dark when there is light there?

Solution: Both "fire" and "darkness" are powerful figures of speech which appropriately describe the unthinkable reality of hell. It is like fire because it is a place of destruction and torment. Yet, it is like outer darkness because people are lost there forever. While hell is a literal place, not every description of it should be taken literally. Some powerful figures of speech are used to portray this literal place. It's horrible reality, wherein body and soul will suffer forever, goes far beyond any mere figure of speech that may be used to describe it. But, it is a serious mistake to take a figure of speech literally. By doing so, one can conclude that God has feathers, since He is described as having wings! (Ps. 91:4). There are other figures of speech used to describe the eternal destiny of the lost that, if taken literally, contradict each other. For example, hell is depicted as an eternal garbage dump (Mark 9:43-48), which has a bottom. But, it is also portrayed as a bottomless pit (Rev. 20:3). Each is a vivid depiction of a place of everlasting punishment. [The Big Book of Bible Difficulties: Clear and Concise Answers from Genesis to Revelation]

Their *Duration*

forever - the nightmare of these false teachers will never end! The specified duration of hell:

- Everlasting punishment: Matthew 25:46.
- Eternal condemnation: Mark 3:29 (sin).
- Eternal judgment: Hebrews 6:2.
- Everlasting destruction: II Thessalonians 1:9.
- Eternal fire: Matthew 18:8–9. ("Gehenna"); Matthew 25:41; Jude 7.
- Unquenchable fire: Mark 9:43–38 (cf. Isaiah 66:24).

- Eternal torment: Revelation 19:20; 20:10.

So we have seen the Way of these false teachers: They are as Deceptive as Submerged rocks; Disappointing as lying Skies; Dead as Stone-dead trees; Destructive as a Savage Storm; and Doomed as a Shooting Star. Let's be clear, the way of these false teachers is not so obvious, as we confronted them, without the discernment of the Scriptures. One verse comes to mind that we would do well to take to heart: Beloved, do not believe every spirit, but test the spirits, whether they are of God; because many false prophets have gone out into the world."
1 John 4:1

I am reminded of Carlos Santana who won 8 Grammy awards for his album Supernatural, which has sold more than 10 million copies. A recent Rolling Stone profile of Santana describes Santana's spirituality:

"His meditation spot is in front of the fireplace.... A card with the word Metatron is spelled out in intricately painted picture letters lies on the floor next to the fireplace. Metatron is an angel. San-tan-a has been in regular contact with him since 1994. Carlos will sit here facing the wall, the candles lit. He has a yellow legal pad at one side, ready for the communications that will come. "It's kind of like a fax machine," he says...There are few conversations with [San-tan-a] that don't lead to discussion of angels, or of the spiritual radio through which music comes. Santana has been increasingly engaged by angels since the day in 1988 when he picked up a book on the subject at the Milwaukee airport. "It's an enormous peace, the few times I have felt the presence in the room," he says...."My reality is that God speaks to you every day. There's an inner voice, and when you hear it, you get a little tingle in your me-dulla oblongata at the back of your neck, a little shiver, and at two o'clock in the morning, everything's really quiet and you meditate and you got the candles, you got the incense and you've been chanting, and all of a sudden you hear this voice: Write this down. It is just an inner voice, and you trust it. That voice will never take you to the desert...."

Sounds enlightening, doesn't it? He is so popular, He even mentions God, His way seems so right - But the truth is, it is nothing short of communicating with demons, which the Bible strictly warns us against. We must apply the Word of God, testing the spirits of all who claim to give good guidance. If a person doesn't line up with the Scripture, do not follow his ways.

THE *WARNING* AGAINST FALSE TEACHERS

Many residents of Washington remember exactly where they were and what they were doing on the morning Mount St. Helen's blew wide-open. The shock wave rattled windows for hundreds of miles around. Prior to the eruption, scientists monitoring the peak didn't know when it would go off or how big the blast would be. But all the signs of a live volcano were evident. It was just a matter of time. Local media issued warnings and faithfully reported St. Helen's vital signs. But as time elapsed and the big eruption did not occur, people became less wary and more bold. Campers, photographers, and others moved in to get a closer look. Then on May 18, 1980, the mountain that had been dormant since 1857 spewed ash skyward and killed at least thirty people. They had failed to heed warnings, and they died needlessly. God has been warning false teachers along time - way back in the days of Enoch, the 7th from Adam! But the warning has gone unheeded, as we still have false teacher, alive and well in our day.

14 *It was* also about these men *that* Enoch, *in* the seventh *generation* from Adam, prophesied, saying, "Behold, the Lord came

with many thousands of His holy ones, ¹⁵ to
execute judgment upon all, and to convict all
the ungodly of all their ungodly deeds which
they have done in an ungodly way, and of all
the harsh things which ungodly sinners have
spoken against Him." Jude 1:14-15

THERE IS A WARNING *ABOUT* THEM

It was also about these men that Enoch, in the
seventh generation from Adam, prophesied -
Enoch was a great man of God:

He was *True* to God

"21 Enoch lived sixty-five years, and begot
Methuselah. 22 After he begot Methuselah,
Enoch walked with God three hundred years,
and had sons and daughters. 23 So all the
days of Enoch were three hundred and sixty-
five years. 24 And Enoch walked with God;
and he was not, for God took him." Genesis
5:21-24

The basic idea of walking with God is holiness.
God is holy, and those who would have
fellowship with him must be holy as well. John
declares this in his first letter:

"This is the message we have heard from him
and declare to you: God is light; in him there

is no darkness at all. If we claim to have fellowship with him yet walk in the darkness, we lie and do not live by the truth. But if we walk in the light, as he is in the light, we have fellowship with one another, and the blood of Jesus, his Son, purifies us from all sin" (1 John 1:5-7).

He *Trusted* God

"5 By faith Enoch was taken away so that he did not see death, "and was not found, because God had taken him"; for before he was taken he had this testimony, that he pleased God. 6 But without faith it is impossible to please Him, for he who comes to God must believe that He is, and that He is a rewarder of those who diligently seek Him. Hebrews 11:5-6

Faith in that passage is an unwavering belief that God is Real and that He is a Rewarder of those who seek Him.

He *Testified* for God (Jude 14)

Enoch was a preacher who warned people that when his son Methuselah died, the flood would come! God apparently revealed this to Enoch, as he named his son Methuselah. The name Methuselah comes from two roots: muth, a root that means "death." Muth = death occurs 125 times in the O.T. Another is shalach meaning "to bring, or to send forth." Thus when he died it shall bring forth. This is confirmed by the fact that when Methuselah died, the flood came! Methuselah was 187 when he had Lamech, and lived 782 years more. Lamech had Noah when he was 182 [Gen.5:25-28]. The flood came in Noah's 600th year [Gen.7:6, 11]. Add it up: 187 + 182 + 600 = 969 the year Methuselah died [Gen.5:27]. This also reveals the tremendous mercy and patience of God, in that Methuselah is the oldest man in the Bible.

Philips, "Enoch was a prophet. The name he gave to his son, "Methuselah," foretold the coming of judgment in his own day and age. It means "when he dies, it shall come." Sure enough, although Methuselah lived longer than any other human being, when he died, the Flood came. But Enoch saw beyond his own day and age to another apostate age—ours. He saw the end-times coming of the Lord. The original vision was embedded in the first prophecy ever given on this planet: "I will put enmity between thee [the serpent] and the woman, and between thy seed and her seed; it shall bruise thy head, and thou shalt bruise his heel" (Gen. 3:15). This prophecy, spoken by God in the Garden of Eden, embraced both comings of Christ. Enoch not only believed the prophecy but also plumbed its depths and expanded on its second coming aspect. "Behold," he said, "the Lord cometh with ten thousands of his saints..." Enoch, like all of the other Old Testament prophets, had no vision of or information regarding the church age. Therefore, he ignores the rapture of the church, about which he knew nothing, because it was not the direct subject of Old Testament revelation and he concentrates on the coming of Christ at the very end of the age to reign. With the full light of New Testament revelation in our hands, we now know that, before the Lord comes with His saints, He will first come for His saints (1 Thess. 4:13-5:9; 2 Thess. 2:6-8).

He was *Translated* by God

McGee, "We know from the record in Genesis that Enoch was translated, that is, he was removed from the earth without dying. And sometime in the future, the church, meaning true believers, is to be removed from the earth without dying. Of course, through the centuries since the time of Christ, believers have been dying so that at the present time most of the church has already passed through the doorway of death. And at the time of the Rapture they are to be caught up together with the living believers to meet the Lord in the air. This teaching is not in the Old Testament at all, yet Enoch is a type or a representative of the believers who will take part in the Rapture. Enoch was removed from the earthly scene before the judgment of the Flood came upon the earth. And the believers who compose the true church will be removed from this earth, will be caught up to meet the Lord in the air, before the judgment of the Great Tribulation breaks upon the earth."

THERE IS A WARNING *TO* THEM

The Lord is *Coming*

The *Certainty*

Behold the Lord came with - [lit., came, indic. aor] - MacArthur, "The first certainty is that the Lord will come (cf. Dan. 7:13; Luke 12:40; Acts 1:9-11; 1 Thess. 3:13). The aorist tense of the verb translated came suggests Enoch's vision was so startling and convincing that he spoke as if the judgment had already occurred. The certainty of Christ's return was under attack from the false teachers, and Jude's reminder reinforced the apostle Peter's earlier teaching on this matter (cf. 2 Peter 3:1-10)." Reminded me of a family that was returning from Church after the morning

Service. The preacher had preached on the Second Coming of Christ. The family was discussing it - the teenage boy had a lot of questions about it. The man tried to answer all of his questions but concluded with, "Son, the best way to prepare for it, is to live each day as if it were your last."
The teenager said, "Remember, I tried that once, and you grounded me for a month!"

The *Company*

with many thousands of His holy ones – this word can refer to the angels (Deut. 33:2; Matt. 25:31). Or to God's people (Revelation 19:14; Colossians 3:4; and 1 Thessalonians 3:13), more than likely here it refers to both.

The *Condemning*

It will be *Unpleasant*. [for the lost]

to execute judgment - In 1992, after years of eluding the police, Mafia boss John Gotti finally was convicted of murder and other organized crimes and was sentenced to life in prison. He had previously thought himself immune to the law. Nicknamed "The Teflon Don" for escaping punishment by bribing jurors, Gotti enjoyed a life of luxury. He ate at the best restaurants, wore the most expensive suits, and had his hair trimmed daily by his personal barber. But Gotti ultimately learned that justice comes in the end. After compiling enough evidence to convict him, the FBI convinced his under-boss, Salvatore Gravano, to testify against him in court. On June 24, 1992, Gotti was sentenced and taken to Marion, Illinois, the most secure federal prison. For eight years, he spent nearly 24 hours a day in a concrete 7-by-8-foot cell with a radio, a small television, a cot, a basin, and a toilet. He was allowed two showers a week, and he got his meals through a slot in the cell door. Speaking in prison to his relatives, Gotti conceded, "I'm cursed. I'm stuck in this joint here, and that's the end of it." In 1998, Gotti was diagnosed with cancer and he died in January 2002, soon he will be experiencing a judgment that will make that prison seem like paradise!

It will be *Unavoidable*

upon all...all...all...all - big shots, little shots, and those that ought to be shot! None outside of Christ can escape. Soon after Saddam Hussein's capture—out of an 8-foot hole that one observer said was filled with rats and mice—he was flown to a secret location for a meeting with 4 members of Iraq's Governing Council. They wanted to confirm that it was indeed Saddam Hussein. When the men were offered the chance to see Saddam through a window or by camera, they said, "No, we want to talk to him." Despite his condition, Saddam was defiant and unrepentant. Ahmad Chalabi, the head of the Iraqi National Congress, said: "He was quite lucid. He had command of his faculties. He would not apologize to the Iraqi people. He did not deny any of the crimes he was confronted with having done. He tried to justify them." "The world is crazy," said one of the council members in the room. "I was in his torture chamber in 1979, and now he was sitting there powerless in front of me without anybody stopping me from doing anything to him, just imagine. We were arguing, and he was using very foul language." The four men spent about 30 minutes in the small room, confronting Saddam with his crimes. As they left, one council member spoke these final words to the former dictator: "May God curse you. Tell me, when are you going to be accountable to God and the Day of Judgment? What are you going to tell him about the mass graves, the Iran-Iraq war, thousands and thousands executed? What are you going to tell God?"

Everyone outside of Jesus Christ will face wrathful judgment.

It will be on the *Ungodly*

who are ungodly...ungodly...ungodly... - "The prefix "un" means to be without. Joined to the word "godly," it means that the person, the nation or the subject under consideration is without God. The ungodly person may appear to be beautiful in character, attractive in manner, cultivated, refined and educated, but they are living without God. He has no faith in God, and may be rebellious toward God. He may be quite religious in his outward actions, and yet have no knowledge personally of Jesus Christ. Such a person is un-godly."
[A Dictionary of Bible Types]

It will be *Unpardonable*

have spoken against Him - you can reject anybody and everybody on the planet - except one - and be saved. That one is the Lord Jesus Christ!

Kismaker "Jude indicates that these men will be convinced because of the evil acts they have committed and the harsh words they have spoken against the Lord...They deliberately taunt God, dishonor Him, and scorn His Word."

They are like Pharaoh who said, "Who is the LORD, that I should obey His voice to let Israel go? I do not know the LORD, nor will I let Israel go." Exodus 5:2

God is still giving a warning about and to the false teachers. Unfortunately many are still flirting with unbelievable danger. The Winter 1991 issue, of the University of Pacific Review, gave a chilling description of the 1986 Chernobyl nuclear disaster:

"There were two electrical engineers in the control room that night, and the best thing that could be said for what they were doing is they were 'playing around' with the machine. They were performing what the Soviets later described as an unauthorized experiment. They were trying to see how long a turbine would 'free wheel' when they took the power off it. Now, taking the power off that kind of a nuclear reactor is a difficult, dangerous thing to do, because these reactors are very unstable in their lower ranges. In order to get the reactor down to that kind of power, where they could perform the test they were interested in performing, they had to override manually six separate computer-driven alarm systems. One by one the computers would come up and say, 'Stop! Dangerous! Go no further!' And one by one, rather than shutting off the experiment, they shut off the alarms and kept going. You know the results: it was the largest industrial accident ever to occur in the world.

- Chernobyl accident is equivalent to 500 nuclear bombs used in Hiroshima in 1945.
- The releases contaminated an estimated 17 million people to some degree.
- 143,000 people have been evacuated from contaminated areas of Ukraine
- 600,000 people took part in liquidating effects of the disaster, 100,000 of which already died or are now handicapped
- Cases of leucosis and thyroid cancer exceed average by 2 and 5 times correspondingly among the Chernobyl victims
- There are 1.8 million people residing on the territories of Ukraine, Russia, and Belarus, which are still defined as contaminated.
- For the 14 years since the disaster 300,000 died in Ukraine alone from the radiation sickness.

That's nothing compared to the fall out that will occur when God judges all of the false teachers that had lead people astray through human history!

Chapter Five

Defense against the Ungodly

17 But you, beloved, ought to remember the words that were spoken beforehand by the apostles of our Lord Jesus Christ, 18 that they were saying to you, "In the last time there will be mockers, following after their own ungodly lusts." 19 These are the ones who cause divisions, worldly-minded, devoid of the Spirit. 20 But you, beloved, building yourselves up on your most holy faith, praying in the Holy Spirit, 21 keep yourselves in the love of God, waiting anxiously for the mercy of our Lord Jesus Christ to eternal life. 22 And have mercy on some, who are doubting; 23 save others, snatching them out of the fire; and on some have mercy with fear, hating even the garment polluted by the flesh. Jude 1:17-23

During a practical exercise at a military police base, the instructor was giving the class instruction in unarmed self-defense. After he presented a number of different situations in which they might find themselves, he asked a student, "What steps would you take if someone were coming at you with a big, sharp knife?" The student replied. "BIG ones!"

We have in the rest of this book seven big steps we can take in our Defense against the ungodly: (1) Remembering God's Precepts; (2)Recognizing the need for Prayer; (3) Remaining in His Passionate love; (4) Realizing the Lord's Promise; (5)Reaching out to those who are Perishing; (6) Relying on His Power; and (7) Responding with Praise.

REMEMBERING THE *WORDS* OF THE *APOSTLES*

They *Foster Reassurance*

But you, beloved - how do we know that we are beloved? Would you get this from our performance? From these false teachers? From our circumstances? From our Feelings? No! We get reassurance from knowing that we are loved, because God's Word says so! "Beloved!" That term of endearment is for the believer, not for the apostate. It is one of the names that God gives to His own. We are "believers," "disciples," "Christians," and "brothers." Above all, we are God's beloved. It was His own name for His Son (Eph. 1:6). It was the name by which Barnabas was known (Acts 15:25)—and Amplias and Persis (Rom. 16:8, 12), and Tychicus (Eph. 6:21), and Onesimus (Col. 4:9), and Luke (Col. 4:14), and Apphia and Philemon (Philem. 2), and Paul (2 Peter 3:8), and Timothy (2 Tim. 1:2). It is the name used for all believers (1 Thessalonians 1:4/1 Cor. 15:58). Jude uses the term 4 times in this little letter: 1:1, 3, 17, 20. We should note that any love we have for God, is based on the fact that He first loved us, "We love Him because He first loved us." 1 John 4:19. How much does God love us?

'I in them, and You in Me; that they may be made perfect in one, and that the world may know that You have sent Me, and have loved them as You have loved Me." John 17:23

Major Sullivan Ballou, of the Union Army, to his wife Sarah:

"Sarah, my love for you is deathless. It seems to bind me with many cables that nothing but Omnipotence can break. And yet my love of country comes over me like a strong wind and bears me irresistibly with all those chains to the battlefield. The memory of all those blissful moments I have enjoyed with you come crowding over me, and I feel most grateful to God and you that I have enjoyed them for so long. And how hard it is for me to give them up and burn to ashes the future years, when God willing, we might have loved and lived together, and watched our boys grow up around us to honorable manhood. If I do not return my dear Sarah, never forget how much I loved you nor that when my last breath escapes me on the battlefield it will whimper your name." One week later, Major Ballou was killed at the first battle of Bull Run. It demonstrates the power of remembering love on the battlefield - as we are battling with the ungodly; we do well to remember that we are Beloved...by God Himself!

Richard Halverson, "There is nothing you can to do make God love you more! There is nothing you can do to make God love you less! His love is Unconditional, Impartial, Everlasting, Infinite, Perfect!"   Again we only know this because God's Word tells us!

"35 Who then can ever keep Christ's love from us? When we have trouble or calamity, when we are hunted down or destroyed, is it because he doesn't love us anymore? And if we are hungry or penniless or in danger or threatened with death, has God deserted us? 36 No, for the Scriptures tell us that for His sake we must be ready to face death at every moment of the day—we are like sheep awaiting slaughter; 37 but despite all this, overwhelming victory is ours through Christ who loved us enough to die for us. 38 For I am convinced that nothing can ever separate us from His love. Death can't, and life can't. The angels won't, and all the powers of hell itself cannot keep God's love away. Our fears for today, our worries about tomorrow, 39 or where we are—high above the sky, or in the deepest ocean—nothing will ever be able to separate us from the love of God demonstrated by our Lord Jesus Christ when He died for us." Romans 8:35-39 (TLB)

They should be *Firmly Remembered*

remember - this is the first commandment given in this letter. We need to remember God's Word (2 Peter 3:1-2). But we cannot remember something that we have never known any more than we can remember someone whom we have never met. It is important, then, that we lay a good foundation in the Word. God expects us to know, study, and memorize His Word (Joshua 1:8 /Job 23:12). When we choose to be in God's House hearing the Word instead of going out to eat Sunday afternoon, we will be making spiritual progress (Psalm 119:10-11/Jeremiah 15:16 /Colossians 3:16). In March 2007, the American Idol television competition was nearing its final weeks. Haley Scarnato, age 24, from San Antonio, Texas was one of the contestants. During the first week of the finals, each of the contestants had to sing a song made famous by singer Diana Ross. Diana was a guest-judge during that week of competition and helped coach the contestants.One of the first to perform that night was Brandon Rogers. Soon after he began, Brandon forgot the words to the song "You Can't Hurry Love" and stood there in silence smiling. Haley Scarnato performed a bit later in the evening. Haley chose the song "Missing You", but halfway through her performance she too forgot the lyrics, but kept going until she was able to remember the rest of the song. One of the last performers of the night was Stephanie Edwards. She chose the song "Love Hangover" and she also forgot some of the words, but was able to finish her song. It was an unusual night where three of the twelve performers could not remember the words to the songs they were singing. Truth is, if we are going to finish well in this contest with false teachers we need to remember God's Word.

It reminded me of the owner's manual, you get when you buy a gadget or an appliance. Normally, at the back of the manual is a "Trouble-shooting" guide. In that guide, you will likely find a list of solutions to any problems you might be experiencing. In the same sense, the Christian believer has been given a trouble-shooting guide for correcting the problems that false teachers bring into the church. If we carefully follow the instructions found in God's Word, then our church can remain sound in doctrine until the Lord Comes for us.

They are God's Full and Final Revelation

the words that were spoken beforehand by the apostles of our Lord Jesus Christ - the church revolved around the apostles doctrine (Acts 2:42). Why? Their doctrine was the inspired Word of God! And notice it was "spoken" a past tense, not something that is ongoing. Jude 3, "once and for all delivered unto the saints." It is foundational truth and you only need lay a foundation once (Ephesians 2:20). Adding, subtracting from, or neglecting God's Word only gives false teachers a foothold in our lives.

THE *WARNING* ABOUT THE *APOSTATES*

Warning about their *Lips*

[18] *that they were saying to you, "In the last time there will be mockers* - We have already looked at this.

Warning about their *Lives*

following after their own ungodly lusts -
we have seen this also under their depiction.

Warning about their *Loss*

*These are the ones who cause divisions,
worldly-minded, devoid of the Spirit -* the
word sensual is translated "natural" in 2 Cor.
2:14. While all believers are indwelt with the
Holy Spirit, lost people are not. God's Word
warns us about coming apostates.

Swindoll, "The apostles words alert the
troops...so that the sudden assault of the
apostates won't take them by surprise. The
infiltration of mockers who follow after their
own ungodly lusts comes with the territory of
the last times. In defending the borders of the
faith, we are to keep a vigilant watch with our
binoculars, scanning the horizon for enemy
movement." See Acts 20:29-31/1 Timothy
4:1/2 Timothy 3:1-9 /2 Timothy 4:2-4. We
would be wise to heed the warning and realize
there is trouble up head. Argentinean race
driver Juan Manuel Fangio discovered that
after the opening lap of the 1950 Monaco
Grand Prix. as he approached a dangerous
bend for the second time, that something was
wrong. The faces of the spectators, which he
usually saw as a whitish blur as he drove by,

were all turned away from him. He later said, "I thought if they are not looking at me, they must be looking at something more interesting around the corner." So he braked hard and carefully rounded the bend, where he saw that his split second assessment had been accurate. The road was blocked by a massive pileup.

ALLOWING THE *WORKING* OF GODS AS IT *ABIDES*

But you, beloved, building yourselves up on your most holy faith - The believer builds upon the foundation of holy faith. What does this mean? By faith is meant our beliefs, the body of truth that we have learned from Scripture. It is the Holy Scripture that tells us about God and His Son, the Lord Jesus Christ, and about man and his world. This is significant, for it means that our beliefs are not our own opinions nor the opinions of any other man. Our beliefs come directly from Jesus Christ and the Holy Spirit of God as they inspired prophets to write the Holy Scripture. This is probably what Jude meant by holy. Remember holy means separate, set apart, and different. Our holy faith is far different from all other faiths. It is a faith that is not based upon opinion, speculation, or imaginations of men.

It is faith that has been separated and set apart from man's ideas about God and life. It is a faith that is separated and set apart by God Himself which has come from God. It is the "most holy faith" of God, His Son, and His Spirit—the holy faith that is to be held by all the people of the earth. The point is this: believers are to build up their lives upon their holy faith. They are to study, meditate, learn, memorize, and live out the Scripture. They are to build upon what they have learned and then continue to build more and more. The only way believers can do this is to continually study the holy faith, the living Word of God. [Teacher's Outline and Study Bible - Commentary]

Butler, "The believer must never stand still spiritually. He must always be growing. A growing person is a healthy person. A healthy person is better able to fight off attacks to his body by germs. So it is spiritually. To grow spiritually, the believer must be much in the Word and prayer." See Acts 20:32 /1 Peter 2:2.

One notes, "Turning away from God's Word is the defiant first step toward apostasy. It also marks the beginning of eroding morals...The first step in character conservation is a step back into God's Word." The best defense against Apostates, is not to study what they believe, but to Remain in the words of the Apostles. The American Banking Association has a training program... Each year it sends hundreds of bank tellers to Washington in order to teach them to detect counterfeit money, which is a great source of a loss of revenue to the Treasury Department. "It is most interesting that during the entire two-week training program, no teller touches counterfeit money. Only the original passes through his hands. The reason for this is that the American Banking Association is convinced that if a man is thoroughly familiar with the original, he will not be deceived by the counterfeit bill, no matter how much like the original it appears."

RECOGNIZING THE NEED FOR PRAYER

The transatlantic telegraph cable was the first cable used for telegraph communications laid across the floor of the Atlantic Ocean. It bridged North America and Europe, and expedited communication between the two. Whereas it would normally take at least ten days to deliver a message by ship, it now took a matter of minutes by telegraph. One wrote, "But what is the Atlantic cable, compared with the heavenly cable of prayer, whereby the tempted and tried man communicates with the

God of heaven, and receives messages of encouragement from heaven." Another great line of Defense against false teachers is prayer. Our first line of defense is Remembering God's Precepts; now Recognizing the need for Prayer (Jude 20b)

NOTICE THE *CONTRAST*

The false teachers are those "not having the Spirit" and thus cannot possibly "pray in the Spirit." Lost people's prayers are not honored by God! The Spirit only works through Jesus Christ (Jn.14:6).

"For through Him we both have access by one Spirit to the Father." Ephesians 2:18

"Therefore, brethren, having boldness to enter the Holiest by the blood of Jesus," Hebrews 10:19

"For the eyes of the LORD are on the righteous, And His ears are open to their prayers; But the face of the LORD is against those who do evil." 1 Peter 3:12

For there is one God and one Mediator between God and men, the Man Christ Jesus," 1 Timothy 2:5

A gang of prisoners in a Brazilian jail spent months digging a tunnel in a bid for freedom. But they emerged from the tunnel's end still inside the prison yard! The underground escape route, which had reportedly taken 67 men months to complete, ended just 1 foot short of the main perimeter wall. Prison guards promptly took the discouraged prisoners back to their cells. Man can try and try to free himself from the prison of self, and work his way to God - but all to no avail. Coming to God is only accomplished as the Holy Spirit applies the work of Christ to our heart.

NOTICE THE *CONNECTION*

Prayer is connected with God's Word:

"But you, beloved, building yourselves up on your most holy faith",...God's Word, and "praying in the Holy Spirit," Jude 1:20

"If you abide in Me, and My words abide in you, you will ask what you desire, and it shall be done for you." John 15:7

"but we will give ourselves continually to prayer and to the ministry of the word." Acts 6:4

"17 And take the helmet of salvation, and the sword of the Spirit, which is the word of God; 18 praying always with all prayer and supplication in the Spirit, being watchful to this end with all perseverance and supplication for all the saints-- 19 and for me, that utterance may be given to me, that I may open my mouth boldly to make known the mystery of the gospel, Ephesians 6:17-19

"4 For every creature of God is good, and nothing is to be refused if it is received with thanksgiving; 5 for it is sanctified by the word of God and prayer. 1Timothy 4:4-5

"12 For the word of God is living and powerful, and sharper than any two-edged sword, piercing even to the division of soul and spirit, and of joints and marrow, and is a discerner of the thoughts and intents of the heart...16 Let us therefore come boldly to the throne of grace, that we may obtain mercy and find grace to help in time of need. Hebrews 4:12, 16

Bounds notes, "The Word of God is a great help in prayer. If it be lodged and written in our hearts, it will form an out-flowing current of prayer, full and irresistible. Promises, stored in the heart, are to be the fuel from which prayer receives life and warmth, just as the coal, stored in the earth, ministers to our comfort on stormy days and wintry nights. The Word of God is the food, by which prayer is nourished and made strong. Prayer, like man, cannot live by bread alone, "but by every word which proceedeth out of the mouth of the Lord." Unless the vital forces of prayer are supplied by God's Word, prayer, though earnest, in its urgency, is, in reality, flabby, and void. The absence of vital force in praying can be traced to the absence of a constant supply of God's Word, to renew the life. He who would learn to pray well, must first study God's Word, and store it in his memory and thought."

A *CONTINUATION*

praying - a pres. Tense, speaking of continual action. We must pray without ceasing because the warfare never ceases!

"Then He spoke a parable to them, that men always ought to pray and not lose heart," Luke 18:1

The diary of George Mueller, Christian social reformer from the Victorian era, chronicles his devotion in prayer:

"In November 1844, I began to pray for the conversion of five individuals. I prayed every day without a single intermission, whether sick or in health, on the land, on the sea, and whatever the pressure of my engagements might be. Eighteen months elapsed before the first of the five was converted. I thanked God and prayed on for the others. Five years elapsed, and then the second was converted. I thanked God for the second, and prayed on for the other three. Day by day, I continued to pray for them, and six years passed before the third was converted. I thanked God for the three, and went on praying for the other two. These two remained unconverted."

Thirty-six years later he wrote that the other two, were still not converted. He wrote:

"But I hope in God, I pray on, and look for the answer. They are not converted yet, but they will be."

In 1897, 52 years after he began to pray, these two men were finally converted, after he died.

The repeated intercessions of Abraham for Sodom and Gomorrah present an example of persistent praying; Jacob, wrestled all night with the angel of the Lord, saying, "I will not let go until you bless me." Moses prayed forty days and forty nights, seeking to stay the wrath of God against Israel; Elijah repeatedly prayed 7 times before the raincloud appeared above the horizon; and on one occasion Daniel pressed his case 3 weeks, before the answer and the blessing came. Many nights during His earthly life the Lord Jesus spent in prayer. In Gethsemane He presented the same petition, three times; Paul prayed three times about his thorn in the flesh. 7 "Ask, and it will be given to you; seek, and you will find; knock, and it will be opened to you. 8 For everyone who asks receives, and he who seeks finds, and to him who knocks it will be opened." Matthew 7:7-8

A *CONFESSION*

in the Holy Spirit - implies our weakness and our need for the Spirit's help.

"Likewise the Spirit also helps in our weaknesses. For we do not know what we should pray for as we ought, but the Spirit Himself makes intercession for us with groanings which cannot be uttered." Romans 8:26

- First, the Holy Spirit is our Companion, He Resides in us (Rom. 8:9).
- Furthermore, the Spirit understands our Condition, He Rescues us. He "helps in our weakness", it carries the idea of coming to someone's aid, to rescue them. "And in like manner also the Spirit lends us a helping hand with reference to our weakness, for the particular thing that we should pray for according to what is necessary in the nature of the case, we do not know with an absolute knowledge; but the Spirit himself comes to our rescue by interceding with unutterable groanings.
- Moreover, He who is constantly searching our hearts knows what is the mind of the Spirit because, according to God, He continually makes intercession on behalf of the saints. Romans 8:26 (WuestNT)
  "So too the [Holy] Spirit comes to our aid and bears us up in our weakness; for we do not know what prayer to offer nor how to offer it worthily as we ought, but the Spirit Himself goes to meet our supplication and pleads in our behalf with unspeakable yearnings

and groanings too deep for
utterance." Romans 8:26 (AMP)

Reminds me of a Commercial, by Woods,
Snively & Associates. "Sometimes bad things
happen to good people. When justice hangs in
the balance; when life has taken an awful
turn; when your problems are too big to
handle and your opponents are even bigger.
Let the experienced trial lawyers at Woods,
Snively & Associates help you level the playing
field, and bring justice back to your side.
Whether you've been in a car wreck; need a
divorce; or have a loved one in jail. Our
experienced team of litigators who concentrate
in these areas, are here to help you. No
matter what your problem is, our team of
lawyers are dedicated and aggressive. We're
here to help you - call us, if you don't call, we
can't help." We can say, "Sometimes
seemingly bad things happen to blood bought,
Christ-imputed children of God. Life is often
unjust and takes an awful turn. Problems
become to big too handle; and you have fierce
Satanic opponents. Whether you've been in a
car wreck, been divorced, have a loved one
who is in jail, or whatever you're facing - your
fault or not! God's grace through Christ is
available to you. All God's Spirit does, as far
as you need to be concerned, is concentrate
on your life. He is within you to help. No

matter what your problem He is dedicated and aggressive. He is within you to help - call upon the name of the Lord, if you don't call, He will not help."

One of our defenses is Prayer. Swindoll, "Jude is exhorting the troops to readiness. They are to stay in shape, keep in close communication with headquarters and watch vigilantly for the coming of their Commander in Chief...Praying in the Holy Spirit is an admission of our weakness...When we acknowledge our weakness, depend on the Holy Spirit to bridge this gap, and have a spirit submissive to God's will...we are praying in the Spirit. We are never so strong as when we are in prayer. Kneeling knees don't knock!"

REMAINING PASSIONATE **IN** *LOVE*

A group of professionals asked the question, "What does love mean?" to a group of 4 to 8 year olds. Here are some of the answers:

- Tommy, age 6, said, "Love is like a little old woman and a little old man who are still friends even after they know each other so well."

- Mary Ann, age 4, said, "Love is when your puppy licks your face even after you left him alone all day."

- Mark, age 6, said, "Love is when Mummy sees Daddy on the toilet and she doesn't think its gross."

It is amazing when you think about it, in spite of the fact that we often neglect God; in spite of the fact that he knows us - our true motives our failures and sins; in spite of the fact that He sees us at our worst, undignified moments; He still passionately loves us! We must keep that truth ever in our minds...Defense against false teachers involves Remaining in His Passionate Love.

THE *DEMAND*

keep yourselves - it means to watch carefully, guard; keep, hold in reserve, preserve; observe, obey, pay attention to. What we should keep:

(1) Keep from the paths of the destroyer (Ps. 17:4).
(2) Keep the heart diligently (Prov.4:23).
(3) Keep the sayings of Christ (John 8:51-2)
(4) Keep the commandments of Christ (John 14:15)
(5) Keep the unity of the spirit Ephesians 4:3
(6) Keep our body under control (1 Cor.9:27)
(7) Keep pure (1 Tim.5:22)
(8) Keep the faith (2 Tim.4:7)
(9) Keep unspotted from the world James

1:27
(10) Keep yourself from idols. 1 Jn. 5:21).
(11) In our passage, Keep in the love of God
Jude 21

We are commanded to keep ourselves in God's love. On several occasions I have planted sun flowers. I notice they follow the sun. That is what we need to do, follow God's love for us! A believer is nurtured as he is occupied with God's love for him, and is in fellowship with Him. Hudson Taylor was interviewing some young people who had volunteered for the foreign missionary field. He asked them, "Why do you wish to go as a foreign missionary?" One said, "I want to reach others across the sea because Christ has commanded us to go into all the world and preach the Gospel to every creature." Another said, "I want to go because millions are dying without ever having heard of Jesus, the only One who can save them." Others have similar answers. Hudson Taylor "All of your motives are good, but I fear they will fail you in times of severe testing and tribulation—especially if you are confronted with the possibility of having to face death for your testimony. The only motive that will enable you to remain true is stated in 2 Cor. 5:14. Christ's love constraining you will keep you faithful in every situation."

"Now may the Lord direct your hearts into the love of God and into the patience of Christ." 2 Thessalonians 3:5

"The grace of the Lord Jesus Christ, and the love of God, and the communion of the Holy Spirit be with you all. Amen." 2 Corinthians 13:14

Philips, "When we engage the apostate in battle, we are in peril, not so much of being convinced by his arguments but of allowing bitterness, dislike, hostility, anger, and the like to spring up in our hearts. We are apt to forget that the poor, lost man whom we are opposing is a dupe, a tool of the Evil One. Even when He was denouncing in the strongest terms the apostate leaders of Israel who were plotting His crucifixion, the Lord Jesus never stopped loving them. He made every effort to reach the conscience of Judas, even when the wretched man, sitting at the Lord's table with the Lord and His people, had the blood money in his purse. Hence, the need to "keep" ourselves in the love of God."

THE *DESCRIPTION*

in the love of God - Kismaker, "The phrase the love of God can mean either God's love for man or man's love for God...the context seems to favor God's love for man. As Jude states in the salutation in verse 1, the readers "are loved by God the Father." God comes to man and surrounds him with divine love." Now we need to stay in that sphere of love.

McShane, "His love flows on fresh and full as a river, but...[we must] make sure that nothing, not even our contending for the faith, will in any way rob us of our consciousness of it. All know only too well that dealing with evil and disputing with heretics can have a hardening effect upon the heart and smother within it the warmth and joy of the love of God. The Lord taught His disciples to abide in His love and continue in it (Jn. 15:9-10). It has been bestowed upon us (1 Jn. 3:1), and it has been "shed abroad in our hearts by the Holy Spirit" (Rom.5:5). While here it is not our love to God, yet whatever love is present in our hearts toward Him is but the reflection of His love to us."

Love is agape - Jude is not suggesting that we keep ourselves in such a way that we earn the love of God. God loves us with an unconditional love (John 3:16, John 15:13, Romans 5:8). God's love for us is not based on what we do. He loves us regardless. Such is the nature of God (1 Jn.4:8; 4:16).

Sorenson says, "The primary verb in this lengthy sentence is keep which is also an imperative. The basic thought thus is to keep ourselves in the love of God..." The idea is that we need to cultivate the love of God in our own hearts. God is never going to stop loving us. Nothing or no one is going to separate us from His love."

See Rom. 8:31-39/Eph. 3:17-19. Remaining in His Passionate Love, a few years ago we just had a terrific snow storm for this part of the country. There were several days when I did not see the sun - but that sun was always shining! On Wednesday there was snow up to my knees, no sun in sight. But they forecasted that by Sunday, the sun was to be shining and the temperature was supposed to be near 60 degrees. I kept myself in the sun, by knowing it was still there, still shining somewhere and in a few days it would break through! God's love is always shining, even when we cannot see or feel it, just wait in the hope that it will break through any moment!

REALIZING THE LORD'S PROMISE TO RETURN

It is said that two kinds of birds fly over the California deserts: the hummingbird and the vulture. All the vulture can see is rotting meat because that is all he looks for. He thrives on that diet. But the hummingbird ignores the carcasses and the smelly flesh of dead animals. Instead, he looks for the tiny blossoms of the cactus flowers. He buzzes around until he finds the colorful blooms almost hidden from view by the rocks. Each bird finds what it is looking for. While we acknowledge that there are, and will be, false teachers in the Church. We should not be looking for them as our focus; we should be looking for the Lord to meet us in the air - that is to be our focus. Defense against the ungodly by realizing the Lord's promise to return. So we have, Remember God's Precepts; Recognize the need for Prayer; Remaining in His Passionate love, now Realizing the Lord's Promise to Return (Jude 21).

THE *EXPECTATION*

waiting anxiously for the mercy of our Lord Jesus Christ to eternal life - The New Testament uses this Greek word most predominantly to mean "await." There are those who waited for Christ at his First coming, such as Simeon (Lu. 2:25); and Anna (Lu. 2:38). We are waiting for the Rapture, expecting it at any moment!

"so that you are not lacking in any spiritual gift, as you wait for the revealing of our Lord Jesus Christ, 1 Corinthians 1:7 (ESV)

"20 But our citizenship is in heaven, and from it we await a Savior, the Lord Jesus Christ, 21 who will transform our lowly body to be like His glorious body, by the power that enables Him even to subject all things to Himself." Philippians 3:20-21 (ESV)

"waiting for our blessed hope, the appearing of the glory of our great God and Savior Jesus Christ, Titus 2:13 (ESV)

"7 Be patient, therefore, brothers, until the coming of the Lord. See how the farmer waits for the precious fruit of the earth, being patient about it, until it receives the early and the late rains. 8 You also, be patient. Establish your hearts, for the coming of the Lord is at hand." James 5:7-8 (ESV)

We have to be patiently doing what God called us to do as we wait for him to Return. We have won the spiritual lottery and are just waiting to cash in. Reminds me of Joe Treala, he tried to get on the Jeopardy show, several times, but was never invited on the show. But he didn't give up, he kept trying to get on a game show and finally his patience paid off. Joe, a resident of Gilroy California, got on the "Who Wants to Be a Millionaire" show. Joe took his time answering the many questions. It took him 15 minutes to answer one of the questions. He said, "The producers were getting kinda cranky with me," But in the end, his patient ways paid off for him-a million different ways. He worked his way to the million dollar question, which was, "What insect shorted out an early supercomputer and inspired the term, "computer bug?" The answer "moth" was worth a million dollars to the 25-year-old computer customer service representative. We have to patiently expect the Lord to Return, and at that time we will all be winners of something far greater than a mere million dollars! After all no amount of money can (1) remove the sin nature; (2) or purchase the New Jerusalem; or (3) buy a glorified body; or (4) bring forth the joy of perfect, uninterrupted fellowship with God Himself.

IT WILL BE AN *EXPRESSION* OF MERCY.

for the mercy of our Lord Jesus Christ - "For although they were to build themselves up, and to pray in the Holy Spirit, and keep themselves in the love of God, yet this building, praying, and keeping, cannot merit heaven; for, after all their diligence, earnestness, self-denial, watching, obedience, etc., they must look for the MERCY of the Lord Jesus Christ, to bring them to ETERNAL LIFE." [A Commentary and Critical Notes].

It will be mercy that causes us to avoid going through the Tribulation Period - we are not going to be removed because we do not deserve God's wrath; but because in mercy, Jesus took the wrath that we deserve, by dying as our substitute on the cross.

"Because you have kept my word about patient endurance, I will keep you from the hour of trial that is coming on the whole world, to try those who dwell on the earth." Revelation 3:10

It will be mercy, in that we will not get what we deserve at the Judgment Seat of Christ. "so Christ, having been offered once to bear the sins of many, will appear a second time, not to deal with sin but to save those who are eagerly waiting for him." Hebrews 9:28

Peter Lord, former pastor told of a junior high school boy who was always in trouble. So much so that he was actually called "a troublemaker." The boy's parents were called to come to school to meet with the principle and the young man's teacher. They arrived and braced themselves for bad news. The teacher began, "Thanks for coming. I just wanted to share with you a list of 10 positive and beneficial things about the known "Troublemaker." When the teacher finished, the parents bracing themselves said, "And what else - give us the bad news." The teacher said, "That's all I wanted to say!" They went home and shared that word with the boy and he changed immediately. Satan wants you to think, that God views you as a Troublemaker, one who can't wait to give you some bad news after the rapture. But all God is going to share with you is positive and beneficial! It is only then when many of us we see just how good, the good news really is! The bad news of our sin was heard at Calvary!

THE *EXHILARATION* OF SALVATION COMPLETION

that leads to eternal life - eternal life has many aspects.

Ungers, "This is a priceless treasure, the gift of God. It is not to be confused with mere endless existence, which all possess, saved as well as unsaved. Christ said, "I came that they might have life, and might have it abundantly" (John 10:10). This life is nothing less than "Christ in you, the hope of glory" (Col. 1:27). It is likened to a birth from above (John 3:3; John 1:13) and is dependent upon receiving Christ as Savior. "He who has the Son has the life; he who does not have the Son of God does not have the life" (1 John 5:12).

Eternal life must not be confused with natural life. This form of life is subject to death and is derived by human generation. Spiritual life has a beginning but no end. The difference is that one possessing mere natural life will be separated eternally from God in the lake of fire, whereas the one possessing eternal life will be united and in fellowship with God for all eternity. Thus, separation from God is eternal death; union with God is eternal life." [The New Unger's Bible Dictionary]

Eternal life is a Present possession of every believer:

"14 And as Moses lifted up the serpent in the wilderness, so must the Son of Man be lifted up, 15 that whoever believes in him may have eternal life. 16 "For God so loved the world, that he gave his only Son, that whoever believes in him should not perish but have eternal life." John 3:14-16

"Whoever believes in the Son has eternal life; whoever does not obey the Son shall not see life, but the wrath of God remains on him." John 3:36

Eternal life is also a Promise to be realized in glory:

"28 And Peter said, "See, we have left our homes and followed you." 29 And he said to them, "Truly, I say to you, there is no one who has left house or wife or brothers or parents or children, for the sake of the kingdom of God, 30 who will not receive many times more in this time, and in the age to come eternal life." Luke 18:28-30

Or think of it this way, eternal life from a Past perspective, is deliverance from sin's penalty, which is immediate, secured by Christ's death Rom. 1:16; Acts 28:18, 16:31; Rom. 10:10; 1 Cor. 15:2; 2 Tim. 1:9. This also includes deliverance from sin's power, Heb. 7:25; Rom. 5:9; James 1:23; 1 Tim. 4:6; Phil. 2:12. Eternal life from a Future perspective will be deliverance from sin's very presence,

Rom. 13:11; Heb. 9:28; Phil. 3:20; 1 Thess. 5:8

Dwight L. Moody said:

"I was down in Texas some time ago, and happened to pick up a newspaper, and in it they called me "Old Moody." Honestly, I had never been called old before. I went to my hotel, and looked in the looking glass. I can't conceive of getting old. I have a life that is never going to end. Death may change my position but not my condition, not my standing with Jesus Christ. "Old! I wish you all felt as young as I do here tonight. Why, I am only sixty-two years old! If you meet me ten million years hence, then I will be young. Read that ninety-first Psalm, 'With long life will I satisfy him.' That doesn't mean seventy years. Would that satisfy you? "Did you ever see a man or woman of seventy satisfied? Don't they want to live longer? You know that seventy wouldn't satisfy you. Would eighty? Would ninety? Would one hundred? "If Adam had lived to be a million years old, and then had to die, he wouldn't be satisfied. 'With long life will I satisfy him'—life without end! Don't call me old. I am only sixty-two. I have only begun to live."

Realizing the Lord's Promise to Return keeps us keeping on. Because of erosion, the historic Cape Hatteras Lighthouse was in peril of washing into the Atlantic Ocean. So Congress appropriated $12 million for the National Park service to move it 2900 feet to safety. With a combination of care, expertise, patience and raw power, The Expert House Movers of Sharptown, Maryland moved the 208 foot tall, 9.7 million pound structure to its current location. The option of moving the lighthouse was first proposed in April of 1982, but the light wasn't lit at its new location until November 13, 1999. Seventeen years of study and 23 days of moving later. I do not know how much, the combined weight, of every believer that will go up in the rapture will be; but we are patiently waiting for it to happen - How by God's wisdom and power! He has promised to move us from this corrupt world, to our new home. We are to expectantly look for that to happen one of these days. Dwight L. Moody used to say, "I never preach a sermon without thinking that possibly the Lord may come before I preach another."

G. Campbell Morgan, the distinguished British clergyman said, "I never begin my work in the morning without thinking that perhaps God may interrupt my work and begin His own. I am not looking for death. I am looking for Him."

Martin Luther said he only had two days on his calendar—today and "that day."

Dr. Horatius Bonar, as he drew the curtains at night and retired to rest, used to repeat to himself the words, as if in prayer, and certainly with expectancy, 'Perhaps tonight, Lord!' In the morning, as he awoke and looked out on the dawn of a new day, he would say, looking up into the sky. 'Perhaps today, Lord!' He expected the Lord to return at any moment. Bonar was in the Lord's service for over 60 years.

REACHING OUT TO THOSE WHO ARE PERISHING

Fanny Crosby, the blind song writer, was at the McAuley Mission. She asked if there was a boy there who had no mother, and if he would come up and let her lay her hand on his head. A little fellow came up, and she put her arms about him and kissed him. That incident inspired her to write the song, "Rescue the Perishing."

Rescue the perishing, care for the dying, snatch them in pity from sin and the grave; weep o'er the erring one, lift up the fallen, tell them of Jesus, the mighty to save.
Refrain:
Rescue the perishing, care for the dying; Jesus is merciful, Jesus will save.

Years later, when Mr. Sankey was about to sing the song in St. Louis, he related this incident. A man sprang to his feet in the audience and said, "I am the boy she kissed that night. I never was able to get away from the impression made by that touching act, until I became a Christian. I am now living in this city with my family, and I am a Christian." Our hearts should go out to those who are perishing, to the point where we are willing to share the gospel with them.

Defense against the ungodly - Reaching out to those who are Perishing. Defense, (1) Remembering God's Precepts; (2) Recognizing the need for Prayer; and Rescue the Perishing (Jude 22-23).

"There is a debate whether there are 3 groups of people or just 2 groups. The NIV presents 3 groups:

"22 Be merciful to those who doubt; 23 snatch others from the fire and save them; to others show mercy, mixed with fear--hating even the clothing stained by corrupted flesh. Jude 1:22-23 (NIV)

So you would have (1) those who are hesitating or doubting; (2) those who need to be saved from the fire; and (3) those who need mercy because they are contaminated. This is possible, NKJ/NAS/ESV present it as if addressing two groups. The Greek text is very difficult to nail down.

THE *DOUBTERS*

Their *Need*

And have mercy - imper. pres. act. Ling. Key to the Greek NT, "To show pity, to be merciful, to see someone in dire need and to have compassion and try to help them."

"24 And the Lord's servant must not be quarrelsome but kind to everyone, able to teach, patiently enduring evil, 25 correcting his opponents with gentleness. God may perhaps grant them repentance leading to a knowledge of the truth, 26 and they may come to their senses and escape from the snare of the devil, after being captured by him to do his will." 2 Timothy 2:24-26

It is debated whether we are talking about a saved person who is being persuaded by these false teachers; or a lost person who is considering the teaching of the false teachers. Either way, they both need mercy. We cannot treat people according to what they deserve! They do not need justice but mercy. Salvation is totally undeserved; it is a gospel of mercy for the miserable.

"And as Jesus passed on from there, two blind men followed him, crying aloud, "Have mercy on us, Son of David." Matthew 9:27

"21 And Jesus went away from there and withdrew to the district of Tyre and Sidon. 22 And behold, a Canaanite woman from that region came out and was crying, "Have mercy on me, O Lord, Son of David; my daughter is severely oppressed by a demon." Matthew 15:21-22

"said, "Lord, have mercy on my son, for he is an epileptic and he suffers terribly. For often he falls into the fire, and often into the water. Matthew 17:15

"9 He also told this parable to some who trusted in themselves that they were righteous, and treated others with contempt: 10 "Two men went up into the temple to pray, one a Pharisee and the other a tax collector. 11 The Pharisee, standing by himself, prayed thus: 'God, I thank you that I am not like other men, extortioners, unjust, adulterers, or even like this tax collector. 12 I fast twice a

week; I give tithes of all that I get.' 13 But the tax collector, standing far off, would not even lift up his eyes to heaven, but beat his breast, saying, 'God, be merciful to me, a sinner!' 14 I tell you, this man went down to his house justified, rather than the other. For everyone who exalts himself will be humbled, but the one who humbles himself will be exalted."
Luke 18:9-14

"5 he saved us, not because of works done by us in righteousness, but according to his own mercy, by the washing of regeneration and renewal of the Holy Spirit," Titus 3:5

The Lost need mercy, while we are to be merciful by giving them the Gospel, only God can ultimately grant mercy!

"15 For he says to Moses, "I will have mercy on whom I have mercy, and I will have compassion on whom I have compassion." 16 So then it depends not on human will or exertion, but on God, who has mercy."
Romans 9:15-16

The ungodly do not deserve mercy, but that is the gospel we offer them. Hamilton took the gospel to cannibals in Africa; as a result he was murdered and eaten! Later his two sons went to the same place and lead many to

Christ. They actually shared communion with the men who had digested their fathers flesh! Those men didn't deserve salvation, but these boys understood mercy. But there are also believers who get confused and have doubts and are deceived by false teachers...they need mercy also.

"3 But I am afraid that as the serpent deceived Eve by his cunning, your thoughts will be led astray from a sincere and pure devotion to Christ. 4 For if someone comes and proclaims another Jesus than the one we proclaimed, or if you receive a different spirit from the one you received, or if you accept a different gospel from the one you accepted, you put up with it readily enough." 2 Corinthians 11:3-4

"1 O foolish Galatians! Who has bewitched you? It was before your eyes that Jesus Christ was publicly portrayed as crucified. 2 Let me ask you only this: Did you receive the Spirit by works of the law or by hearing with faith? 3 Are you so foolish? Having begun by the Spirit, are you now being perfected by the flesh? 4 Did you suffer so many things in vain—if indeed it was in vain?" Galatians 3:1-4

"11 And he gave the apostles, the prophets, the evangelists, the shepherds and teachers,

12 to equip the saints for the work of ministry, for building up the body of Christ, 13 until we all attain to the unity of the faith and of the knowledge of the Son of God, to mature manhood, to the measure of the stature of the fullness of Christ, 14 so that we may no longer be children, tossed to and fro by the waves and carried about by every wind of doctrine, by human cunning, by craftiness in deceitful schemes." Ephesians 4:11-14

Their *Nature*

on those who are doubting -   There is a variant, some have it "doubt" while a variant has it "dispute, or a distinction (NKJ). Most translations go with "doubt." [NAS/ESV/NIV/WUEST]

Barclay, "There are those who are flirting with falsehood. They are obviously attracted by the wrong way and are on the brink of committing themselves to error, but are still hesitating before taking the final step. They must be argued out of their error while there is time."

MacDonald, "The Scripture makes a distinction between the way we should handle those who are [leaders] of false cults and those who have been duped by them. In the case of the leaders, the policy is given in 2 Jn. 10-11. But in speaking of those who have been deceived by false teachers...we should show a compassionate interest in them and try to guide them out of doubts into a firm conviction of divine truth."

THE *DEFILED*

The *Possibility*

save others - those who have committed themselves to false teaching. Notice they are not beyond hope - cult members can be saved. Again this can refer to saving a lost soul or delivering a believer from a cult.

"19 My brothers, if anyone among you wanders from the truth and someone brings him back, 20 let him know that whoever brings back a sinner from his wandering will save his soul from death and will cover a multitude of sins." James 5:19-20

The *Urgency*

snatching them out of the fire - "I overthrew some of you, as when God overthrew Sodom and Gomorrah, and you were as a brand plucked out of the burning; yet you did not return to me," declares the LORD. Amos 4:11

"1 Then he showed me Joshua the high priest standing before the angel of the LORD, and Satan standing at his right hand to accuse him. 2 And the LORD said to Satan, "The LORD rebuke you, O Satan! The LORD who has chosen Jerusalem rebuke you! Is not this a brand plucked from the fire?" Zechariah 3:1-2

Swindoll, "Flirting with falsehood is playing with fire. When we reach out to those engulfed in flames of apostasy, we may grab them uncomfortably by the scruff of their necks, but we will save their lives from certain destruction."

Sometime we have to be aggressive in dealing with people, Dwight L. Moody once saw a man freezing to death on the street in Chicago. Moody could not just talk this man into warmth. He pounded him with his fist and got him really angry. The man began to pound back and then got up and ran after Moody. That got his blood circulating and saved his life. Our loud and outspoken witnessing may make people angry, but at least it may awaken them from their spiritual stupor. John Wesley's father, Samuel, was a pastor, but there were those in his parish who did not like him. On February 9, 1709, a fire broke out in the rectory at Epworth, possibly set by one of the rector's enemies. Young John, not yet 6 years old, was stranded on an upper floor of the building. Two neighbors rescued the lad just seconds before the roof crashed in. One neighbor stood on the other's shoulders and pulled young John through the window. Samuel Wesley said, "Come, neighbors, let us kneel down. Let us give thanks to God. He has given me all my 8 children. Let the house go. I am rich enough." John Wesley often referred to himself as a "brand plucked out of the fire" (Zech 3:2; Amos 4:11). In later years he often noted February 9 in his journal and gave thanks to God for His mercy.

The *Cautionary*

on some have mercy with fear – one observes, "The second half tells us how to approach people in need: mercifully and with fear. There is always certain danger for the sinner, but there is also the risk of danger to the rescuer. A physician who reaches out to cure a disease-ridden patient always runs the risk of infection."

"Jesus said to them, "Watch and beware of the leaven of the Pharisees and Sadducees." Matthew 16:6

Do not be deceived: "Bad company ruins good morals." 1 Corinthians 15:33

False teachers can influence more then we realize. Jamie Rouse commenting on how the music affected his behavior said, "I used to think, This ain't affecting me, you'd have to be weak-minded to let this stuff affect you, and the whole time it affected me." Jamie Rouse is the student who, on November 15, 1995, walked into his Lynnville, Tennessee, high school carrying a .22 caliber rifle and killed a teacher and a student.

The *Mentality*

hating even the garment polluted by the flesh - as one said we are to love the sinner, while hating the sin. We are to hate some things!

"8 But of the Son he says, "Your throne, O God, is forever and ever, the scepter of uprightness is the scepter of your kingdom. 9 You have loved righteousness and hated wickedness; therefore God, your God, has anointed you with the oil of gladness beyond your companions." Hebrews 1:8-9

"For I do not understand my own actions. For I do not do what I want, but I do the very thing I hate." Romans 7:15

"Yet this you have: you hate the works of the Nicolaitans, which I also hate. Revelation 2:6

As one said we are to love the sinner, while hating the sin. J.B. Mayor, "While it is the duty of the Christian to pity and pray for the sinner, he must view with loathing all that bears traces of the sin." In the OT the clothing of a leper was contaminated and needed to be burned.

"47 "When there is a case of leprous disease in a garment, whether a woolen or a linen garment, 48 in warp or woof of linen or wool, or in a skin or in anything made of skin, 49 if the disease is greenish or reddish in the garment, or in the skin or in the warp or the woof or in any article made of skin, it is a case of leprous disease, and it shall be shown to the priest. 50 And the priest shall examine the disease and shut up that which has the disease for seven days. 51 Then he shall examine the disease on the seventh day. If the disease has spread in the garment, in the warp or the woof, or in the skin, whatever be the use of the skin, the disease is a persistent leprous disease; it is unclean. 52 And he shall burn the garment, or the warp or the woof, the wool or the linen, or any article made of skin that is diseased, for it is a persistent leprous disease. It shall be burned in the fire." Leviticus 13:47-52

"Yet you have still a few names in Sardis, people who have not soiled their garments, and they will walk with me in white, for they are worthy." Revelation 3:4

Like saving a drowning person, you have to be careful you don't go under in the process.

Point is that those who are deceived must be confronted - whether saved or lost! According to the Chicago Tribune, a Detroit bus driver finished his shift on the Route 21 bus and headed for the terminal. But somehow he took a wrong turn.
He didn't arrive at the terminal at the scheduled time of 7:19 p.m., and a short time later his supervisors started looking for him. Meanwhile the driver's wife called the terminal and reported her husband might be disoriented from medication he was taking. For 6 hours, the forty-foot city bus and its driver could not be found. Finally the state police found the bus and driver—200 miles northwest of Detroit. The bus was motoring slowly down a rural two-lane road, weaving slightly from side to side. The police pulled the bus over, and the driver said he was lost. A police news release later stated, "The driver

had no idea where he was and agreed he had made a wrong turn somewhere. Apparently this had not occurred to him during the 4 hours he drove without finding the bus depot." We must mercifully confront those who have taken a wrong turn in life.

RELYING UPON GOD'S POWER

Martin Luther was born on Nov. 10, 1483 in Germany. The most powerful hymn of the Reformation, was written by Martin Luther. The hymn is a battle cry which Martin Luther wrote based on Psa. 46:

"1 God is our refuge and strength, A very present help in trouble. 2 Therefore we will not fear, though the earth should change And though the mountains slip into the heart of the sea; 3 Though its waters roar and foam, Though the mountains quake at its swelling pride. Selah."   Psalm 46:1-3

From that hymn, Martin Luther wrote the wonderful hymn, "A Mighty Fortress is our God." Martin Luther said, "I have been so inspired by these words that I have written a hymn based on this text. I also adapted some familiar music for these lines. And these musical truths have become the great rallying cry for our German people. How my soul thrills whenever I hear our people sing this hymn - in unison and with great spiritual fervor. And today you can go to the tomb of Martin Luther at Wittenberg and find these words engraved:

A Mighty fortress is our God,
A bulwark never failing;

Luther knew, as few of us ever will, what it is like to be opposed by the ungodly, he learned the value of relying on God's power.
Defense against the ungodly - Relying upon God's Power. Let's review - (1) Remember the Precepts; (2) Recognizing the need for Prayer; (3) Remaining in His Passionate love; (4) Realizing the Lord's Promise to Return; Rescuing the Perishing; now Relying upon God's Power.

Now to Him who is able to keep you from stumbling, and to make you stand in the presence of His glory blameless with great joy. Jude 24

THE *PRINCIPLE*

Now to Him who is able - the first word in the Greek is "To The One now." Emphasizing how important God is, He alone is the source of our power. *Able* - Verb, pres. tense, δύ-ναμ-αι, doo-nam-I, it is to express ability and capacity to accomplish something in deed, attitude, or thought...He is the Almighty God, with Ability to do anything He chooses to do.

"And when Abram was ninety years old and nine, the Lord appeared to Abram, and said unto him, I am the Almighty God." (Genesis 17:1)

"1 Then Job answered the LORD and said, 2 "I know that You can do all things, And that no purpose of Yours can be thwarted." Job 42:1-2

"Once God has spoken; Twice I have heard this: That power belongs to God;"   Psalm 62:11

 "'Ah Lord GOD! Behold, You have made the heavens and the earth by Your great power and by Your outstretched arm! Nothing is too difficult for You," Jeremiah 32:17

"But Jesus... said unto them... with God all things are possible." (Matthew 19:26)

"For with God nothing shall be impossible." (Luke 1:37)

"And I heard as it were the voice of a great multitude, and as the voice of many waters, and as the voice of mighty thunderings, saying, Alleluia: for the Lord God omnipotent reigneth." (Revelation 19:6)

Tozer, "God is the source of all the power there is. There isn't any power anywhere that doesn't have God as its source, whether it be the power of the intellect, of the spirit, of the soul, of dynamite, of the storm or of magnetic attraction. Wherever there is any power at all, God is the author of it. And the source of anything has to be greater than that which flows out of it. If you pour a quart of milk out of a can, that can has to be equal to or greater than a quart. The can has to be as big as or bigger than that which comes out of it. The can may contain several gallons, though you may pour out only a quart. The source has to be as big or bigger than that which comes out of it. So if all the power there is came from God—all the power—therefore, God's power must be equal to or greater than all the power there is."

Charles Hodge, "We can do very little. God can do whatever He wills. We, beyond very narrow limits, must use means to accomplish our ends. With God means are unnecessary.

He wills, and it is done. He said, Let there be light; and there was light. He, by a volition, created the heavens and the earth. At the volition of Christ, the winds ceased, and there was a great calm. By an act of the will He healed the sick, opened the eyes of the blind, and raised the dead. This simple idea of the omnipotence of God, that He can do without effort, and by a volition, whatever He wills, is the highest conceivable idea of power, and is that which is clearly presented in the Scriptures."

When Martin Luther was in the throes of the Reformation and the Pope was trying to bring him back to the Catholic Church, he sent a cardinal to deal with Luther and buy him with gold.The cardinal wrote to the Pope, "The fool does not love gold." The cardinal, when he could not convince Luther, said to him, "What do you think the Pope cares for the opinions of a German...[farmer]? The Pope's little finger is stronger than all Germany. Do you expect your princes to take up arms to defend you—you, a wretched worm like you? I tell you no. And where will you be then?" Luther's response was simple. "Where am I now, In the hands of Almighty God"

THE *PROMISE*

For Today

who is able to keep you from stumbling - the verb keep, is an aorist tense. "The word here translated 'keep' is a strong word. It is even impregnated with a strong military flavor, and suggests the picture of an armed force. In the center stands one whose life is threatened by fierce and hostile bands, but by his side stands an invincible Warrior pledged to protect him from all evil." [Expositor's Dictionary]

Previously we were told to "keep ourselves in the love of God." But that was a different Gk word, terein which means "watch." Here, the word is phulasse-in which means to "guard." We must watch, in order to stay close to the Lord; but only He can guard us so we will not stumble. It was used by Xenophon a Greek soldier and rider of a horse which had a sure footing, in order to keep it from stumbling. It was used by Plutarch, a Greek biographer and philosopher of snow steadily falling, and by Epictetus, a Greek Stoic philosopher of a good man who does not make moral lapses. Jude is the only New Testament writer to use it. God is able to keep the Christian "from falling," or keep us "on a solid footing," so as not to be tripped up by the ungodliness of false teachers.

"And now to him who can keep you on your feet, standing tall..." Jude 1:24 (MSG)

David Clotfelter, "Is it conceivable that in spite of all this, [Christians] may still fall away and be lost? Is it possible for God to predestine us to holiness, and yet we do not become holy? Can He adopt us as children and then disown us? Can He give us a guarantee of salvation and then renege on His promise? Is the human will so strong as to overcome divine power? Surely not! What more does God need to say to assure us that He will uphold us to the end?"

"31 What then shall we say to these things? If God is for us, who is against us? 32 He who did not spare His own Son, but delivered Him over for us all, how will He not also with Him freely give us all things? 33 Who will bring a charge against God's elect? God is the one who justifies; 34 who is the one who condemns? Christ Jesus is He who died, yes, rather who was raised, who is at the right hand of God, who also intercedes for us." Romans 8:31-34

God is able to take care of us in this life! His Promises are true, "and being fully assured that what God had promised, He was able also to perform." Romans 4:21

- He *Promises* to uphold the weakest among us, "Who are you to judge the servant of another? To his own master he stands or falls; and he will stand, for the Lord is able to make him stand." Romans 14:4
- He always *Provides* a way out, "No temptation has overtaken you but such as is common to man; and God is faithful, who will not allow you to be tempted beyond what you are able, but with the temptation will provide the way of escape also, so that you will be able to endure it."1 Corinthians 10:13
- He does *Plenty* more then we can even imagine, "Now to Him who is able to do far more abundantly beyond all that we ask or think, according to the power that works within us," Ephesians 3:20
- His *Prayers* guarantees our security, "25 Therefore He is able also to save forever those who draw near to God through Him, since He always lives to

make intercession for them." Hebrews
7:25

Rutherford, "Our hope is not hung upon such untwisted thread as "I imagine so," or "It is likely;" but the cable, the strong rope of our fastened anchor, is the oath and promise of Him who is eternal verity [reality]: our salvation is fastened with God's own hand and Christ's own strength to the strong stake of God's unchanging nature."

F. B. Meyer wrote about two Germans who wanted to climb the Matterhorn. They hired three guides and began their ascent at the steepest and most slippery part. The men roped themselves together in this order: guide, traveler, guide, traveler, and guide. They had gone only a little way up the side when the last man lost his footing. He was kept by the other four, because each had a toehold in the niches they had cut in the ice. But then the next man slipped, and he pulled down the two above him. The only one to stand firm was the first guide, who had driven a spike deep into the ice. Because he held his ground, all the men beneath him regained their footing. F. B. Meyer concluded by saying, "I am like one of those men who slipped, but thank God, I am bound in a living partnership to Christ. And because He stands, I will never perish."

For Tomorrow. [throughout eternity]

and to make you stand in the presence of His glory blameless with great joy - God is able to make or cause us to stand before Him blameless!

"Now to the one who is able to keep you from falling, and to cause you to stand, rejoicing, without blemish before his glorious presence," Jude 1:24 (NET)

In God's glorious presence blameless!

"just as He chose us in Him before the foundation of the world, that we would be holy and blameless before Him. In love." Ephesians 1:4

"yet He has now reconciled you in His fleshly body through death, in order to present you before Him holy and blameless and beyond reproach— " Colossians 1:22

The Christian is in Christ; therefore we are identified with the Blameless One.

"but with precious blood, as of a lamb unblemished and spotless, the blood of Christ." 1 Peter 1:19

The word is Amomos, which was used of a sacrificial lamb that was without spot or blemish and thus could be offered to God.

In March 2006, a city dump truck backed into Curtis Gokey's car. The car was almost totaled. Curtis sued the city of Lodi, California for 3,600 dollars. But it was Curtis who was driving the city dump truck that backed into his personal car! The city dropped the lawsuit, stating that Curtis could not sue himself. The truth is God cannot blame us without blaming Himself! He Himself paid for all of our sins at the cross; and He Himself has clothed us with His righteousness! The result will obviously be great joy!

"Now to Him Who is able to keep you without stumbling or slipping or falling, and to present [you] unblemished (blameless and faultless) before the presence of His glory in triumphant joy and exultation [with unspeakable, ecstatic delight]—" Jude 1:24 (AMP)

The Cotton Patch, "Now to Him who can keep you on your feet and present you at His court, spick-and-span and happy."

In fact until then we never really know pure joy. Until we lose our sin natures, there is always a shadow over all our lives. But one day we will lose our sin nature and experience the unhindered Presence of God.

"You will make known to me the path of life; In Your presence is fullness of joy; In Your right hand there are pleasures forever. Psalm 16:11

"For His anger is but for a moment, His favor is for a lifetime; Weeping may last for the night, But a shout of joy comes in the morning." Psalm 30:5

"Then he said to them, "Go, eat of the fat, drink of the sweet, and send portions to him who has nothing prepared; for this day is holy to our Lord. Do not be grieved, for the joy of the LORD is your strength." Nehemiah 8:10

Spurgeon, Joy springs from God, and has God for its object. The believer who is in a spiritually healthy state rejoices mainly in God himself; he is happy because there is a God, and because God is in his person and character what he is. All the attributes of God become well-springs of joy to the thoughtful, contemplative believer; for such a man says within his soul, "All these attributes of my God are mine: His power, my protection; His wisdom, my guidance; His faithfulness, my foundation; His grace, my salvation." He is a God who cannot lie, faithful and true to His promise; He is all love, and at the same time infinitely just, supremely holy. Why, the contemplation of God to one who knows that this God is his God forever and ever, is enough to make the eyes overflow with tears, because of the deep, mysterious, unutterable bliss which fills the heart. There was nothing in any of the pretended gods of the heathen, to make the heart glad, but there is everything in the character of Jehovah both to purify the heart and to make it thrill with delight."

Martin Luther said he only had two days on his calendar—today and "that day." Chinese officials invaded underground church in 2005, and found a teacher and 30 children. They arrested them and the children began to sing hymns. They were all interrogated and were told to write 100 times "I do not believe in Jesus." Instead, one child wrote "I believe in Jesus today. I will believe in Jesus tomorrow. I will believe in Jesus forever!" Soon the others began to write the same thing! They were told if you do not write "I do not believe in Jesus" 100 times, you will not be released. But the children held firm. Finally the officials called in their parents and scolded them. One official said to a parent, "If you do not deny Jesus, we will not release your son." She said, "Well, I guess you will just have to keep them, because without Jesus, there would be no way for me to take care of them." The exasperated official said, "Take your son and go!"

We need to rely upon God's Power. A Hymn written by Martin Luther says it all!

A mighty fortress is our God,
a bulwark never failing;
our helper he amid the flood
of mortal ills prevailing.
For still our ancient foe
doth seek to work us woe;
his craft and power are great,
and armed with cruel hate,
on earth is not his equal.

Did we in our own strength confide,
our striving would be losing,
were not the right man on our side,
the man of God's own choosing.
Dost ask who that may be?
Christ Jesus, it is he;
Lord Sabbath, his name,
from age to age the same,
and he must win the battle.

And though this world, with devils filled,
should threaten to undo us,
we will not fear, for God hath willed
his truth to triumph through us.
The Prince of Darkness grim,
we tremble not for him;

his rage we can endure,
for lo, his doom is sure;
one little word shall fell him.

That word above all earthly powers,
no thanks to them, abideth;
the Spirit and the gifts are ours,
thru him who with us sideth.
Let goods and kindred go,
this mortal life also;
the body they may kill;
God's truth abideth still;
his kingdom is forever.

Chapter Six

A Doxology

to the only God our Savior, through Jesus Christ our Lord, *be* glory, majesty, dominion and authority, before all time and now and forever. Amen. Jude 1:25

The Duke of Wellington, the British military leader defeated Napoleon at Waterloo. In his old age a young lady asked him what, if anything, he would do differently if he had his life to live over again. Wellington thought for a moment, then replied. "I'd give more praise," If I had my life to live over again - I'd give God more praise. Praise keeps our eyes on God - on Who He is and What He can do. This could go under the last section also, Defense against the Ungodly - Responding with Praise. But let's make it a closing doxology.

PRAISE HIM THAT HE IS *SOLITARY*

To the only God - It means "Only, alone, solitary, no other.

Hezekiah prayed before the LORD and said, "O LORD, the God of Israel, who are enthroned above the cherubim, You are the God, You alone, of all the kingdoms of the earth. You have made heaven and earth. 16 "Incline Your ear, O LORD, and hear; open Your eyes, O LORD, and see; and listen to the words of Sennacherib, which he has sent to reproach the living God. 17 "Truly, O LORD, the kings of Assyria have devastated the nations and their lands 18 and have cast their gods into the fire, for they were not gods but the work of men's hands, wood and stone. So they have destroyed them. 19 "Now, O LORD our God, I pray, deliver us from his hand that all the kingdoms of the earth may know that You alone, O LORD, are God."   2 Kings 19:15-19

"For You are great and do wondrous deeds; You alone are God." Psalm 86:10

"Now, O LORD our God, deliver us from his hand that all the kingdoms of the earth may know that You alone, LORD, are God." Isaiah 37:20

"How can you believe, when you receive glory from one another and you do not seek the glory that is from the one and only God?" John 5:44

"This is eternal life, that they may know You, the only true God, and Jesus Christ whom You have sent. John 17:3

"Now to the King eternal, immortal, invisible, the only God, be honor and glory forever and ever. Amen." 1 Timothy 1:17

C.H. Robinson noted that Jonathan Edwards was suddenly converted, as by a flash of light, in the moment of reading a single verse of the New Testament. He was at home in his father's house; some hindrances kept him from going to church one Sunday with the family. A couple of hours with nothing to do sent him listlessly into the library; the sight of a dull volume with no title on the leather back of it evoked curiosity as to what it could be; he opened it at random and found it to be a Bible; and then his eye caught this verse: "Now unto the King eternal, immortal, invisible, the only wise God, be honor and glory forever and ever. Amen!" (1 Tim. 1:17) "He tells us in his journal that the immediate effect of it was awakening and alarming to his soul, for it brought him a most novel and most extensive thought of the vastness and majesty of the true Sovereign of the universe. Out of this grew the pain of guilt for having resisted such a Monarch so long, and for having served Him so poorly. And whereas he had hitherto had slight notions of his own wickedness and very little poignancy of acute remorse, now he felt the deepest contrition.

"15 which He will bring about at the proper time—He who is the blessed and only Sovereign, the King of kings and Lord of lords, 16 who alone possesses immortality and dwells in unapproachable light, whom no man has seen or can see. To Him be honor and eternal dominion! Amen." 1 Timothy 6:15-16

One of my favorite books is called Gleanings in the Godhead, by Arthur Pink. He has a chapter on the Solitariness of God.

"He is solitary in His majesty, unique in His excellency, peerless in His perfections. He sustains all, but is Himself independent of all. He gives to all and is enriched by none."

PRAISE HIM THAT HE IS *SMART*

Who alone is wise - is found in the NKJ, but not in the NAS/ESV/NIV/WUEST. But it is true that God alone is wise - so we will add it on.

"to the only wise God, through Jesus Christ, be the glory forever. Amen." Romans 16:27

"With Him are wisdom and might; To Him belong counsel and understanding." Job 12:13

"19 Then the mystery was revealed to Daniel in a night vision. Then Daniel blessed the God of heaven; 20 Daniel said, "Let the name of God be blessed forever and ever, For wisdom and power belong to Him." Daniel 2:19-20

"11 And all the angels were standing around the throne and around the elders and the four living creatures; and they fell on their faces before the throne and worshiped God, 12 saying, "Amen, blessing and glory and wisdom and thanksgiving and honor and power and might, be to our God forever and ever. Amen."   Revelation 7:11-12

Tony Evans, "Everything that God constructs, He constructs with that goal in mind. Now remember the ingredients of wisdom. Wisdom is arranging things so they meet a goal in the best way possible. God's wisdom so constructs circumstances and people that they all wind up achieving His goal because there is no higher goal to which they could ever go. God is unique in this. No wonder He is called "the only wise God" (Romans 16:27)! No one else could take all the events of history and so arrange them that they achieve one solitary, all-encompassing purpose. Throughout history, various demagogues, dictators, and madmen have tried to bend history to their will and purpose. But they always fail for at least three reasons. First, they aren't God, even though some of them think they are. Second, because they aren't God, they aren't smart enough to pull off their twisted and grandiose plans for very long. And third, they all die someday. God alone is all-wise. You don't have to embrace God's goal. You don't even have to like it—but God will reach it anyway. You could only stop God from reaching His goal by being greater than He is, by having more attributes than He has. Since most of us know better than to try and checkmate God, we'd be much better off to cooperate with Him in achieving the goal His wisdom has set. When you do this, life begins to come into focus. My youngest son recently started playing football. When he first went out to practice he did not wear his glasses, so things were fuzzy. That meant he was getting up off the ground quite regularly because he was not properly focused on the target. We bought him some athletic glasses, and that brought things in focus. He's not getting hit any less often. The glasses don't prevent bumps and bruises, but now he can see what's coming and know where he's going. That's what wisdom does. Wisdom doesn't mean you don't have problems; it means you can see better. It puts life in a proper focus."

PRAISE HIM THAT HE IS OUR *SAVIOR*

our Savior - speaks of one who delivers or preserves. This can refer to either the Father or the Son. The term Savior appears 24 times in the NT, 16 of which are applied to Jesus Christ and 8 times to God. The Father is the Savior in that He sent His Son to save us from our sin.

"46 And Mary said: "My soul exalts the Lord, 47 and my spirit has rejoiced in God my Savior." Luke 1:46-47

 "For it is for this we labor and strive, because we have fixed our hope on the living God, who is the Savior of all men, especially of believers." 1 Timothy 4:10

Philips, "Apart from God, we poor fallen children of Adam's ruined race have no Savior. God is our Savior. Jesus is our Savior (Matt. 1:21). Jesus is God. There is no getting away from the fact. Yet, the apostate denies it. He denies that he needs a Savior. He denies the deity of Christ. Jude brings us back to basics. The Lord Jesus is "the only wise God our Savior.""

Daniel Webster was dining with a company of literary gentlemen in the city of Boston. A minister of considerable literary reputation sat opposite him at the table, and said, "Mr. Webster, can you comprehend how Jesus Christ can be both God and man?" Mr. Webster said: "No, sir, I cannot comprehend it. If I could comprehend it, He would be no greater than myself. I need a superhuman Savior."

WE PRAISE HIM FOR HIS *SUPREMACY*

through Jesus Christ our Lord - it means "Supreme controller, owner, master, lord." vv. 4, 17, 21, 25

In 2006, a judge in New York allowed Jose Luis Espinal to legally change his name to Jesus Christ. Few of us would be so blatant, but in reality we are all like Jose, because every time we choose to live our lives our way, we are claiming the title "Lord."

Florence Nightingale was born in 1820 in Florence, Italy. Her father was a rich, upper-class well-connected English gentleman.
In 1837, while walking in a garden, Florence had what she described as her 'calling'.
Florence heard the voice of God calling her to do his work, but at this time she had no idea

what that work would be. In 1850, at the age of thirty, Florence wrote in her diary, "I am thirty years of age, the age at which Christ began His mission. Now no more childish things, no more vain things. Now, Lord, let me think only of Thy will." In August 1853, she began to slowly learn her calling. Florence took the position of superintendent at the Institute for the Care of Sick Gentlewomen in London. She began to learn how to become a nurse and she taught others the vocation of nursing. In October 1854, she and 38 other nurses in her charge went to minister during the Crimean War. She was instrumental in getting the conditions of the hospital improved so the wounded would no longer die because of unsanitary conditions. After the war, Florence established the first nursing school. Years later, near the end of her illustrious, life she was asked for her life's secret, and she replied, "Well, I can only give one explanation. That is, I have kept nothing back from God."

WE PRAISE HIM FOR HIS *SPLENDOR*

glory - It means, "Glory, splendor, radiance, fame, renown, honor." Chafer writes, "Glory belongs to Him as light and heat belong to the sun. It therefore becomes a misrepresentation of infinite proportions to withhold from God a worthy acknowledgment of His glory. An injustice is forced upon Him if the entire universe of created beings does not ascribe to Him that essential glory. To fail to do so is to "lie, and do not the truth" (cf. 1 John 1:6). The declarative glory of God, on the other hand, is that which His creatures may accord to Him. Unfallen angels and the redeemed in heaven declare His praises forever. Only fallen angels and members of this fallen race withhold glory from God. Such indignity and insult shall be accounted for to Him alone. It is this rebellion within God's universe which the Son of God will judge in time to come. Of the essential glory of God, again, it may be said that His glory is concentrated in Himself. It is because of what He is that glory belongs to Him and only Him. Respecting the declarative glory, furthermore, it may be stated that all His creation, as all His works, declare to a certain degree that glory— "The heavens declare the glory of God" (Ps. 19:1). However, that which concerns the child of God more particularly is the essential glory itself for it will be that which he must ascribe to Him as rightfully His, and this is not difficult to do at all in the light of what He is and has revealed Himself to be."

Two men stood on the shore watching the sun come up out of the sea. One was a merchant from London; the other was the poet, William Blake. As the bright yellow disk of the sun emerged into view, gilding the water and painting the sky with a thousand colors, the poet turned to the merchant and asked, "What do you see?" "Ah! I see gold," replied the merchant. "The sun looks like a great gold piece. What do you see?" "I see the glory of God," Blake answered, "and I hear a multitude of the heavenly host crying 'Holy, Holy, Holy is the Lord God Almighty. The whole earth is full of His glory.'"

WE PRAISE HIM FOR HIS *STATELINESS*

majesty - "regal, lofty, or stately dignity; imposing character; grandeur: majesty of bearing; supreme greatness or authority; sovereignty:"

"And He is the radiance of His glory and the exact representation of His nature, and upholds all things by the word of His power. When He had made purification of sins, He sat down at the right hand of the Majesty on high," Hebrews 1:3

"Now the main point in what has been said is this: we have such a high priest, who has taken His seat at the right hand of the throne of the Majesty in the heavens," Hebrews 8:1 (NASB)

Tozer, "Old Novatian said, "That in the contemplation of God's majesty, all eloquence is done," which is to say that God is always greater than anything that can be said about Him. No language is worthy of Him. He is more sublime than all sublimity, loftier than all loftiness, more profound than all profundity, more splendid than all splendor, more powerful than all power, more truthful than all truth. Greater than all majesty, more merciful than all mercy, more just than all justice, more pitiful than all pity. Nothing anybody can say about Him is enough."

It was the silver anniversary of the coronation of Elizabeth II as Queen of England. Dr. Jack Hayford of California was touring England with his wife. The celebrating, the countryside, and the spirit and enthusiasm of the English people, coupled with the great historical significance of that kingdom, made those two weeks a special time for the Hayfords. As he felt the courage and motivation of the English people, Hayford realized that there was also a deep feeling in their hearts for the royalty who stood with them in dark hours. Suddenly there came to his mind a feeling that Christ wants his church to have such a sense of loyalty and fellowship, because he must be our leader in good times and bad. One word seemed to charge to the forefront: majesty! That word seemed at the moment to represent the glory, excellence, grace, and power of Christ. By comparison, Queen Elizabeth's glory seemed paltry. Dr. Hayford said to his wife: "Take the notebook and write down some words, will you?" He then began to dictate the key, the notes, the timing, and the lyrics to one of the most popular new songs now being sung by Christians everywhere:

Majesty, worship His Majesty!
Unto Jesus be all glory, honor and praise.
Majesty, Kingdom authority,
Flows from His Throne, unto His own, His anthem raise.

WE PRAISE HIM FOR HIS *STRENGTH*

dominion and authory - Kismaker, "The two

attributes, power [dominion] and authority are virtually synonymous.

"Both riches and honor come from You, and You rule over all, and in Your hand is power and might; and it lies in Your hand to make great and to strengthen everyone." 1 Chronicles 29:12

"Once God has spoken; Twice I have heard this: That power belongs to God;" Psalm 62:11

Vance Havner, "We say, "What power Elijah had!" but he had no power in himself, he was simply "THERE," in the place of power. We might say, "What power that radio has!" "What power that electric light has!" But they are very frail contraptions, they are simply in the place of power, connected with the source. When the traffic officer stops you as you drive down the street, it is not his strength that does it; you could drive over him. It is his authority that makes you halt; he represents something greater than himself. So we are nothing in ourselves, but when we are in the place of God's purpose we have His power, and greater is He that is in us than he that is in the world."

WE PRAISE HIM FOR HIS *SELF-EXISTENCE*

before all time and now and forever. Amen - this speaks of His eternality. Being self-existent He is not affected by time. He is BEFORE all time; He is the Always NOW; He is FOREVER.

"From beginning to end, the Bible declares that God is beyond time. That God existed beyond time is clear from the very first verse: "In the beginning God created the heavens and the earth" (Gen. 1:1). Since time does not begin until the universe does, this places God beyond time. Indeed, according to Hebrews, God created time: "In these last days he has spoken to us by his Son... through whom he framed the ages" (Heb. 1:2 Rotherdam). The word ages (Gk: aionos) is not a reference to the material nature of the universe (Gk: kosmos), but to its unfolding temporal periods. In Exodus 3:14 God said to Moses, "I am who I am." this is best taken as a reference to God's self-existence. Jesus sanctioned this meaning when He said, "Before Abraham was born, I am!" (John 8:58). As the self-existent One before anything else existed, God is prior to time (nontemporal). Psalm 90:2 says, "Before the mountains were born or you brought forth the earth and the world, from everlasting to everlasting you are God." Isaiah 57:15 declares, "For this is what the high and lofty One says—he who lives forever...." First Corinthians 2:7 says, "We speak of God's secret wisdom, a wisdom that has been hidden and that God destined for our glory before time began." In Jesus' great high priestly prayer in John 17:5, He declared, "Father, glorify me in your presence with the glory I had with you before the world began." Before the world began is before time began; thus, Jesus is proclaiming God's timelessness. Paul spoke of "this grace [that] was given us in Christ Jesus before the beginning of time" (2 Tim. 1:9). He also spoke of "the hope of eternal life, which God, who does not lie, promised before the beginning of time" (Titus 1:2). The word time (Gk: chronos) is time as we experience it; that is, a succession of changing moments that forms a past, a present, and a future. Christ is said to be before all of this; He is literally eternal (not temporal); He brought the temporal world into existence (John 1:3; Col. 1:16). Hebrews 1:2 informs us that "he has spoken to us by his Son, whom he appointed heir of all things, and through whom he made the universe" (lit: "framed the ages"). Jude 25 proclaims God's eternality in these words: "To the only God our Savior be glory... through Jesus Christ our

Lord, before all ages, now and forevermore!" (emphasis added). God not only created the ages, but He was also before the ages. To be before time and to have made time is not to be in time. Therefore, the Bible teaches that it was not a creation in time, but a creation of time that God accomplished at the beginning." [Geisler's Systematic Theology]

We would do well to let our life be one of Responding to God with Praise. John Wesley was about 21 years of age when he went to Oxford University. He came from a Christian home, and he was gifted with a keen mind and good looks. Yet still not born-again. Once while speaking with a porter, he discovered that the poor fellow had only one coat and lived in such impoverished conditions that he didn't even have a bed. Yet he was an unusually happy person, filled with gratitude to God. Wesley sarcastically joked about the man's misfortunes. "And what else do you thank God for?" The porter smiled, and said, "I thank Him that He has given me my life and being, a heart to love Him, and above all a constant desire to serve Him!" Wesley was deeply moved, and never forgot the lesson.

Many years later, in 1791, John Wesley lay on his deathbed at the age of 88. Despite Wesley's extreme weakness, he began singing the hymn, "I'll Praise My Maker While I've Breath."

www.ingramcontent.com/pod-product-compliance
Lightning Source LLC
LaVergne TN
LVHW051108080426
835510LV00018B/1963